Dear Chris,

Thanks so much for being
such a cornerstone of/for Mark
beautiful music!

Mary Lou

I Solemnly Swear

The Trials and Triumphs of a Local
County Official in Rural Indiana

Mary Lou Leavell Bernett

*Running for public office and serving
as an elected county official in Indiana from
January 1, 1982 through December 31, 1999*

(Pronunciation: Leavell = level)

Copyright © 2020 by Mary Lou Leavell Bernett

All rights reserved. No part of this book may be reproduced in any form or by any electronic or mechanical means, including information storage and retrieval systems, without permission in writing from the publisher, except by a reviewer who may quote brief passages in a review.

The events and conversations in this book have been set down to the best of the author's recollection. Every effort has been made to trace or contact all copyright holders. The author will be pleased to rectify any mistakes brought to her attention at the earliest opportunity.

First paperback edition, November 2020
Ebook edition, November 2020

Book design by Tom Bernett

ISBN 978-0-578-78386-4 (paperback)
ISBN 978-0-578-78902-6 (ebook)

Library of Congress Control Number: 2020920922

Printed in the United States of America

Published by Mary Lou Bernett
Southern Pines, North Carolina
www.clerk50.com

I Solemnly Swear...

CLERK OF THE MARSHALL CIRCUIT COURT
January 1, 1984—December 31, 1991

I, Mary Lou Leavell, solemnly swear that I will support the Constitution of the United States and the Constitution and laws of the State of Indiana, and all local ordinances, and that I will faithfully and impartially perform and discharge the duties of the office of Clerk of the Marshall Circuit Court, according to the law and the best of my ability.

MARSHALL COUNTY AUDITOR
January 1, 1992—December 31, 1999

I, Mary Lou Leavell, solemnly swear that I will support the Constitution of the United States and the Constitution and laws of the State of Indiana, and all local ordinances, and that I will faithfully and impartially perform and discharge the duties of the office of Marshall County Auditor, according to the law and the best of my ability.

CONTENTS

DEDICATIONS iv

FORWARD vi

PROLOGUE viii

PART ONE—HOW IT STARTED

Chapter 1: The Decision 3
Chapter 2: The Primary 8
Chapter 3: The General 19
Chapter 4: The Marys of Marshall County 33
Chapter 5: The Family 39

PART TWO—CLERK OF THE COURTS

Chapter 6: Learning to be a Boss 47
Chapter 7: I Do, I Do, I Do 65
Chapter 8: The Nine Month Process—
            Without the Baby 78
Chapter 9: Here Comes the Judge(s), Attorneys, Plaintiffs,
            Respondents, Defendants, Prosecutor 112
Chapter 10: Meeting People From All Over the State 129
Chapter 11: New Digs Are Necessary 136

PART THREE—MARSHALL COUNTY AUDITOR

Chapter 12: Goodbye Courts Building, Hello
                    County Building 155
Chapter 13: Mary Lou and Her Boys 160
Chapter 14: The Money Managers 176
Chapter 15: Pay the People, Pay the Bills,
                    Pay the Political Sub-Divisions 183

PART FOUR—OTHER STUFF THAT MATTERED

Chapter 16: Meetings, Meetings, and more Meetings 213
Chapter 17: On the Record, Off the Record,
                    Be Very Careful. 226
Chapter 18: Meeting More People From
                    Around the State 232

PART FIVE—LIFE AFTER COUNTY GOVERNMENT
(There really is one)

Chapter 19: And Now, the End Is Near 249
Chapter 20: Lessons I Learned (and There Were Many) 256
Chapter 21: Movin' On Down the Road 261
Chapter 22: Life After Party Politics, Who Knew? 269

EPILOGUE 289

I Solemnly Swear is dedicated to

My late husband, Tom Leavell, for encouraging me to take the chance to run for office and supporting me through the campaigns and while I held office. And to my sons, TJ and Steve, for their patience and support while I spent so many hours at the courthouse and for all the political conversations at the dinner table.

And to

My husband, Tom Bernett, for patiently listening to these stories over and over again, convincing me to finish the project, and the hours of proofing, editing, and publishing needed to actually complete the book. You are my forever hero and best friend.

And to

All of my former deputies—your unfailing loyalty, hard work, and courtesy made me look good and helped me to succeed. Thank you so much.

And to

My friend, and county government mentor, the late Mary B. Haas. Her patience, grace, and wonderful humor guided me through the first eight years and beyond.

And to

All of the hardworking local elected officials in rural areas all over America—who serve their cities, towns, and counties with competency, loyalty, patience, and good humor, for not nearly enough money. I salute you.

FORWARD

County Government in Indiana

*Taken from the National Association of
County Officials History of County Term Limits*

Indiana is a rare case because it has placed term limits for county officials in the state constitution. Article 6, Section 2 of the Indiana Constitution reads as follows:

"There shall be elected, in each county by the voters thereof, at the time of holding general elections, a Clerk of the Circuit Court, Auditor, Recorder, Treasurer, Sheriff, Coroner, and Surveyor, who shall, severally, hold their offices for four years; and no person shall be eligible to the office of Clerk, Auditor, Recorder, Treasurer, Sheriff, or Coroner more than eight years in any period of twelve years."

Only those county offices listed in the state constitution have term limits. An amendment proposed in the 1980s would have removed term limits on county officials in Indiana. However, the measure was defeated, largely because of popular opinion that the office of sheriff, which controls a large portion of county power and funding, should have a term limit.

Term limits in these county offices is the main reason there is so much 'office switching' in Indiana county governments. Most county officials would prefer to run for re-election and continue to serve in the same office. They are experienced, they have a well trained staff, there is better consistency, etc. However, changing office holders often brings in new ideas, and sometimes younger people with more energy and different skills.

What was more unusual was the 'hold over' county offices in the state. Generally, elected officials take office January 1 following their November election. However, in Indiana there are some offices that had delayed starts that varied from three to twelve months. These were different from county to county, and many counties didn't have any holdover offices. No one could ever explain to me why or how these holdover offices came to be, especially with the inconsistency between counties, and various county offices. However, both the clerk and auditor in Marshall County were holdovers, so it was very common for the clerk to run for auditor, or vice versa, at the end of their second term. That eliminated the need for either of them to have to resign their last year in office to move to a different office.

The holdover provisions were removed on July 1, 2005 by Senate Bill 308. This law eliminated all holdover county offices in the entire state.

PROLOGUE

One night in the fall of 1981 while volunteering at the United Way office, I said to a friend, "I need to get a job," while contemplating my lack of employment choices in Plymouth, Indiana.

"You should run for County Clerk," she replied".

"Me, run for office? Are you nuts? Besides, I couldn't beat Mary B."

"Mary can't run again, because of term limits, so she is running for Auditor. Of course you should run; you could do that job."

"Hmmmmm," and I began to wonder......

That conversation launched eighteen of the most interesting, exciting, humbling, frustrating, irritating, stressful, scary, and wonderfully rewarding years of my life.

I ran for public office, I won, I served four terms in two different offices. My life was forever changed. Who would have guessed?

Part 1 - How It Started

"As a leader, it's a major responsibility on your shoulders to practice the behavior you want others to follow."

—Himanshu Bhatia

Chapter 1
The Decision

That conversation suggesting I run for office, took place while a friend and I were preparing the packets for an upcoming United Way fund-raising campaign. I had been active in Republican politics for many years, working on party fundraisers, candidate fundraisers, registering voters, working election polls, etc. I had always supported the other guys—I never even considered that I could be a candidate.

I gave her suggestion some thought, then decided I would run it by my husband just to see what he would say. Although he had also been active in the GOP, his activities were more of supporter to my projects. I was the risk taker in our family, so I thought he would probably just laugh, like I had, and drop it.

But he didn't. He thought about it, then encouraged me to get some more information about the job. Since he was interested, I decided to be interested.

The first person I called had been the Clerk of Courts when we moved to town. She was also a Republican, so I had gotten to know her through GOP activities. She met with me and was very gracious and enthusiastic; and she thought that I should give this decision serious consideration. "You would be perfect for the job", she said. "However, be prepared to work some very long hours, and to work very hard for those hours." Hard work has never been a problem for me, but I wasn't sure about long hours. I still had young children; my youngest son was not yet in school. I decided to continue my research and speak with two friends, both attorneys, about the judicial side of the job. They also were very supportive and encouraging, so I began to think that perhaps this idea had some merit.

But what about a political campaign? How much would it cost, how much time would it take, what exactly would I have to do, and what would be expected of me by the party?

For the answer to that question, Tom and I met with our Republican County Chairman. He explained to us that he would not get involved in a primary election, and although he did not know of another candidate at that time, any resident of the county over age 18 could file for the office. But if I was unopposed in the primary, or had a primary opponent and won, here is the way it would go: 'The Party' would provide campaign materials for each candidate separately, and as a group. They would design and distribute a brochure listing all of the candidates. They would prepare and run newspaper ads and radio spots on our behalf. All of the candidates must participate in each of the parades in the county, as a group, and we would be expected to work at the GOP booth during the county fair and other festivals and fairs over the summer. In September, we would go door to door as a group on Saturdays, distributing campaign materials for each other. The last requirement—the big requirement—each candidate is expected to donate 2% of the gross wages from the office they are seeking, to county party.

Aha—the money. As we all know, every campaign needs money, regardless whether you're running for President of the United States or City Council. It all takes money. And in my case, the first hand stuck out there for money was my local GOP. Good grief—I was supposed to donate before I even had the job! Ah well, we all know that money makes the political world go round—even the local political world.

During those few weeks, while I met and talked with many people who I thought could steer me in the right direction, Tom and I also spent many hours considering the decision and what we should do. It was a major commitment and I would need his support.

Our children also had to be considered: with the timing of the election our youngest son, Steve, would start school in the fall before I took office. That was a plus. Since door to door campaigning is in the afternoons and early evenings when people are home, our oldest son, TJ, could watch Steve until their dad got home. That was a plus. We would have to attend many, many fund raising events all over the county to meet people—all at our own cost. Not such a plus. Again at our own cost, we would have to do our own newspaper advertising, prepare our own campaign materials and handouts, and anything extra that the party was not providing. Not such a plus.

We knew it would be a lot of work, running a county-wide campaign. In 1982, Marshall County was considered a medium-sized county in our state, but there are ten townships, seven incorporated towns, one city, and miles and miles of rural area, (all with dogs in the yard, some friendly, some not so friendly), a population of 42,000 people—and I wanted to meet everyone of them. Although Tom was a self-employed insurance agent and had many policyholders around the county, we knew it was not going to be an easy job.

Finally, one evening after the boys were in bed, we sat down and discussed at length if we should invest the time, money, and energy in this campaign. Since neither of us could read tea leaves, we were well aware of the gamble. After listing all of the pros and cons of campaigning; my working full time and how it would affect our family; my working full time and how it would affect our checking account; and drinking a large, cold bottle of wine—we decided to GO FOR IT AND WIN IT!

The next morning, as I sat in my quiet kitchen and started writing a press release announcing my candidacy, I began to get really, really excited. I had no realistic idea about the campaign, but tons of enthusiasm and a supportive family. So what else do you need? Well, here's what you need: money, energy, patience, persistence, more money, good ideas, good walking shoes, a red, white, and blue wardrobe, and did I mention money?

Our local newspapers were always interested in candidates for local office and generally were very generous with coverage of their announcements, filings, campaigns, etc. I knew it would be to my advantage to announce my intention to run for office as soon as reasonable. The idea behind this strategy was the hope that it would discourage someone else from running who was still just in the 'thinking about it stage.' We decided to plan for early December. It was getting very close to Thanksgiving and I knew that a lot of people would be out of town during that time and wouldn't read the paper. So, after many drafts of my announcement, and making appointments with the local papers to make sure that they would know I was coming, I officially announced my candidacy for Clerk of the Marshall Circuit Court on December 11, 1981. The announcement was carried in both the Plymouth *The Pilot News* and *The South Bend Tribune*. It was pretty impressive coverage in the Pilot, they printed the entire article. The Trib only ran a picture, but since readers were more interested in the ads for good deals on their Christmas shopping, we got pretty good notice.

I announced my intention to run for office in early December, however, actual candidate filing didn't start until February. As in most states, there is a relatively short time period for filing. The clerk needs time to prepare the ballots, and candidates should know within 30 days whether or not they want to run. Since the local papers show up and take pictures of the first few people to file, and my goal was to try to get as much free publicity throughout this campaign as I possibly could (and stay within the law), I was at the Court House before the doors opened at 8:00 am, February 3, 1982. And it worked. There I was at the end of the day on the front page of the Pilot, leaning on the counter listening to the instructions about being a candidate. (We had homework, financial forms, etc to fill out—who knew?) Unfortunately, in that picture, while I was leaning on the counter, it looked like I had my pencil crammed up my nose. This is not a great way to instill confidence that I was the best person for the job to all those voters reading about my candidacy. At this point I was the only candidate for this office, so all I could do was hope that by the time someone else filed and the campaign was in full swing, they would forget the Clerk candidate using the pencil to scratch her nose.

Well, I was committed now—to run for office that is, not to a mental institution. Although sometimes I wondered if I had indeed started myself in just that direction—becoming mentally unbalanced. But, all was well and I was excited about the possibilities of my future.

I was planning to win. At that time there was no opposition. That euphoria only lasted a few weeks until I found myself with an opponent in the Primary. So here we go—the campaign had started. For real.

Chapter 2
The Primary

The Primary election is really the nominating process for each political party. In Indiana, in order to vote in a primary election you must request a particular party ballot (unless you choose to vote only for school board candidates—those are nonpartisan elections). Any potential candidate who meets the requirements for the office they are seeking can file as a candidate for that office. They just need to state on their filing forms which party they want to be affiliated with. Independent candidates must go through a petition process and are not listed on primary ballots.

Many voters don't like the primary process, but the only other way for a party to nominate their candidates is through the caucus procedure, and Indiana election law does not allow that. So, when a person goes to vote, the precinct officials ask them to declare a party, and they are given the appropriate ballot. The actual act of voting in the primary is, of course, secret, but the fact that a person requested a ballot from a certain party is public record. Hence, many voters get 'tagged' as Republican or Democrat when they don't really have a strong affiliation with either party. It is also how candidates know who to target as potential donors and voters.

In Marshall County, after each election, the official voter registration records are marked with an X in the General Election, or an R or D in the Primary election, depending on the ballot choice of that particular voter. Since this is public record, one of the first things I did was check the voting record of my opponent. Turns out, the record reflected that she had always voted D in the primary elections. I couldn't understand why she would file for the Republican nomination when her voting record clearly stated that she was Democrat. It was not until the following year that I would find out why.

Although she was not really a Republican, she was a formidable opponent. She was serving as the Court Administrator in the Marshall Circuit Court, and had worked for the court system for 10 years. She was originally hired by a Democrat judge, but now worked for a Republican judge and he requested that she run on the Republican ticket. Since she was not particularly active in the GOP, she agreed. Obviously, she was very knowledgeable of the job of Clerk of the Court. Her only lack of experience was on the election side—where I had the most experience (little as it was). I often thought if she had been my Democrat challenger, she probably would have won.

My opponent was (and is still) an incredibly nice person. Since I was (and still am) a nice person, I knew the campaign would not get ugly. I was counting on my many years of activities as a Republican to carry me through, especially since she had never been active in the party.

Primary campaigns are very lonely. There is no monetary support from the county party, and certainly no emotional support. Many party members use the 'I can't get involved' excuse because they don't want to have to publicly support one Republican over another. I tried to respect that thinking, but it was very hard when my opponent was a 'former' Democrat and there was no question that my husband and I were long time Republicans. However, I knew I was in this on my own so we proceeded with developing a campaign the best way we knew how—cheaply.

I did have some supporters within the party, so we started putting together the campaign with some good advice and creative ideas. First and foremost in any campaign (with the exception of raising money) is developing name recognition. Since our county was not huge, the best thing to do was use the newspapers as much as possible, and go door to door and meet as many people as possible.

As we all know, every campaign must provide information, informing the voter about all the wonderful attributes of the candidate and why they should be the chosen one. One way to accomplish this task is... the POLITICAL BROCHURE!!

The brochure must have the candidate's picture on the front, the office they are seeking, and any type of clever slogan that you can think of. The inside should provide all kinds of information, preferably about the candidate and why they are the best choice. However, sometimes there just isn't enough to say about the candidate, so even though white space is nice, at some point it turns into blank space and that is not so good. Therefore we filled in with items that we thought the readers, aka voters, would take the time to read: quotes from every Republican's favorite leader, Abraham Lincoln, a list of the duties of the clerk, and of course my personal statement as to what a wonderful job I would do for the citizens. On the back of the brochure are the final obligatory items; a picture of the family (families are a real asset in a campaign), names and ages of the family members (except of course the ages of the parents), and last but certainly not least—the church that the wonderful family attends. However, in my case, I was Catholic and my husband was not, so everybody knew I took the kids to church by myself, but that didn't really matter as along as you belonged to a church.

To save on expenses, my brochure was printed with brown ink on cream glossy paper. It looked nice, but was economical, and most importantly, served the purpose. Throughout the brochure we filled in with my name, and my slogan.

The slogan was created by a policyholder of Tom's. He liked to make buttons for a hobby, so one day he showed up in Tom's office with sample buttons that stated "Mary Lou in 82." They were white with red ink and had two of the GOP elephant symbols on each side. They were really cute, so we decided we would like to have some more. Even though people only wear buttons when you hand them one, many gals will pin buttons on their purse, so it is a good way to get the name out. Also, many people collect campaign buttons so I might have had a chance to go down in history—at least with the pile of other buttons in the shoe box where collector's often keep their campaign button collection. Since this client was also a Republican and a supporter of my campaign, he offered to make 100 buttons for us for just the cost of the materials. I was fortunate to have a name that rhymes with so many things (I still have the name) and many people came to identify me with that slogan: "MARY LOU IN 82."

I knew the slogan idea was successful because the band students that I worked with at Plymouth High School used it. For several years I had volunteered to help the Big Red Band as the choreographer for the Variety Show. I went to the high school to teach the dance routines during band class, which was just before lunch. Since I never left home without my "Mary Lou in 82" button, the kids got very used to seeing it. The final night of the performance was the weekend before the Primary Election. The students in the show introduced the production staff and asked us to come onto the stage. Since I always watched the show from the audience, while I was walking down to the stage after they called my name, the cast spontaneously started chanting "Mary Lou in 82." How about that for a campaign boost—the audience of 900 people was made up of mostly Plymouth residents, parents and family members of the current cast and past casts of the show. I continued working on the Variety Show throughout my career—using lunch hours in the spring to teach dance routines. I worked on the show until my youngest son graduated in 1996. By that time I had been doing if for twenty-five years—and the old bones were starting to feel it, so I gave it up.

Another way we decided to save money was to not hire a professional photographer for the brochure and advertising photos. A friend came to our house and took pictures with his nice 35mm camera (no digital cams or computer editing). We knew printers and newspapers wanted black and white photos (unless you are having a color brochure—way out of our financial league) so it didn't seem like it would be a big deal to get pictures. It wasn't, until it was time for the family picture.

Since we were doing it ourselves, with a volunteer photographer, it was necessary to do the photos in the evening, after work and school. What I forgot to consider was the fatigue factor of my four year-old son. Now my Steve has grown into a fine young man, but he is very independent and not much inclined to care what people think, and he was already that way when he was four. That is not good while you are trying to take a picture of this fine, upstanding, loving family and what you really want is to smack your tired, contrary four year-old into submission... submission that ends with a radiant, happy smile on his face. We finally got a picture where he wasn't exactly making faces in the camera, but his hands were jammed into his pockets, his eyes were glaring, and his mouth was definitely not smiling. We used it anyway.

The nine year-old was more cooperative. Proudly displaying a "Mary Lou in 82" button on his sweater, he was smiling broadly for the camera, just like his Catholic school education was training him to do—behave. I however, was not smiling at the camera, just a small grin, since I was trying my best not to kill my youngest kid, but my husband had a nice smile on his face—because of course he was oblivious to Steve's stubbornness and didn't consider it his problem anyway.

Along with the brochure, all campaigns need a gimmick. Something people will keep around their house or office and actually use, with your name on it. Some candidates hand out emery boards, 6" rulers, pencils, sun visors and baseball caps, etc. I chose to print up cards that listed the precinct polling places.

The purpose of this card was to inform the voting public as to where they would go to vote on election day, just in case they didn't know that already. I thought it was a great idea since it was information that would come from the clerk's office (the very office I was seeking—how original) and often people, especially new voters and those who have moved, don't know where they are supposed to go to vote. Since I didn't want to lose one potential vote I thought this was a pretty slick idea. It had never been done and provided information, not just some useless item to eventually be thrown away. The list was on one side, and the other side had the obligatory picture, the slogan, and the simple statement "Leavell for Clerk." These were done in black and white, the most economical way possible.

My campaign was beginning to come together now, so I just had to decide if there was anything else I would need. Since gaining name recognition is important, we decided to pop for the infamous 'bumper sticker.' Of course, neither one of us had ever really liked bumper stickers on our car, they are too hard to get off, but we were sure that everyone we knew would want one of mine. In order to get the biggest bang for the buck (since our bucks were dwindling) we decided to make them fluorescent orange with black print. The sticker would read "Leavell for Clerk" in the biggest, most obnoxious letters that would fit on a standard size bumper sticker. Besides, these weren't dated, so if I won the Primary I could use them again for the general election.

Now the only thing left was to purchase a name badge for me, and for Tom, to ensure everyone would know who we were as we attended every single, solitary event in Marshall County over the next three months that had more than two people in attendance. When the boys went with us, they dutifully wore a Leavell for Clerk badge—well, Steve did most of the time. Our badges were red, with white print, in keeping with the button colors, and matching most of the clothes I wore.

There is a very fine line between campaigning and getting in someone's face. I didn't particularly like standing outside the door of a function handing out brochures and cards. I always felt like those things were in the way as they went through the food line and had to juggle their plate, drink, silverware, etc. Then the campaign materials ended up in the trash where nobody ever saw them except the clean up committee, and they were too tired to care. Since both of us are very friendly people, and I am an extrovert, we decided our strategy would be to buy the tickets, show up, eat the dinner, lunch, breakfast, whatever and chat with the folks we knew. Since we were wearing name badges the other people would figure out who we were, know that we were interested in their community (we show up for their functions) and maybe pay attention as the campaign wore on and there were newspaper ads, brochures, notices, etc with more information. On the other hand, they may have thought we were just noisy, obnoxious people, who go around advertising who they are—which I guess pretty much describes most candidates for most offices.

Since I was so busy with this campaign I was always eager to attend these functions, especially the dinners, which meant that I didn't have to worry about fixing dinner for my own family. That is a lot of dinners but most of them were fish fries. Of course, back then, we weren't so concerned about saturated fats and calories, not to mention that these are farming communities and everybody eats everything fried anyway, and follows it with homemade pie!! However, It just so happens, I don't like fried fish. Even though I was raised in the days of no meat on Friday for Catholics (or maybe because of it) I never liked fish. I learned to sort of push the fish around on my plate, or if they had nice fresh rolls I would break it into pieces and make fish sandwiches. I usually ate the cole slaw and potato salad, and I always ate the pie, the pie was never a problem at all....

Along with attending fundraisers, another important part of this campaign, for me, was the door-to-door campaign. I think knocking on a stranger's door after dark is a really good way to get yourself shot—especially in rural Indiana. However, back then not many people were home during the day. So I found it most beneficial to campaign after work/school until right before dark. Since I was usually waiting for my older son to get home from school to stay with Steve (I took Steve once, didn't work out. Surprise). Since I didn't really have all that much time, I decided to campaign in the most heavily Republican areas that I could, which did not really include Plymouth, where I lived.

That meant driving to another town before I could start actually knocking on doors, which used up some of my campaign time. In order to effectively use what time I did have, I made sure that I had all my materials prepared and ready ahead of time. I took a portion of my brochures and wrote on them "Sorry I missed you, Mary Lou." Then, if someone wasn't home I would slip it in their door frame and they would know that I had at least tried.

When someone answered the door, I introduced myself and gave them my materials. Sometimes the folks were very friendly and wanted to visit. Sometimes they were not so friendly, or were very specifically for my opponent. Those moments were somewhat awkward. I didn't expect everyone to be for me (well, I really did,), but I did expect everyone to be cordial. Stupid me. I don't know why I didn't see this as a political discussion on their doorstep—some people are just nuts when it comes to talking politics, and many of them live in my county, in the town where I was campaigning at that moment. One time I got blamed for Richard Nixon—like I was personally responsible for him and what he did. Good Grief!!

But most of the time the folks really appreciated how hard I was working to get elected. While I was campaigning door to door I wore a straw campaign hat, with my obnoxious bumper sticker as a hat band, so that people would know why I was walking up and down their streets. I found out later that as people in these small communities were driving around town they would see me out and about. Since I was always wearing that hat, they knew it was me and it gave the illusion that I was all over town campaigning. The comment was often made that "she is really working hard—she is everywhere. If she works that hard to win, she will probably work that hard in the office"—just because of an obnoxious hat. Whatever works.

There is no question that door-to-door campaigning in Indiana is a challenge—especially in the spring—simply because of the weather. Anyone from the Midwest knows that weather is the one thing that can change four times in one day. So it was not at all surprising when I got ready to go out campaigning one day in April and there it was—snow!! I dug out my boots, resurrected my winter coat, scarf, and gloves, and off I went; slogging through snow and slush, trying, but not succeeding, to stay warm while I cheerily greeted people at their door. Instead of talking about the election and my candidacy, all anyone was interested in was the April snow. But again, it showed that I was very serious about my candidacy and my intention to win the race.

As April wound down, and May 3—THE DAY—loomed on the horizon, I continued to do what I had done from the beginning; go to fund raisers, go door-to-door in the Republican areas, run newspaper ads and radio spots, and respond to any speaking engagements I could find. On the Friday before the election, the local paper ran an article listing the key primary races. They listed my race and the 3-way race for a sheriff nominee. They repeated a lot of the biographical information we had all submitted earlier with our announcements. It was a very nice, informative article, but when we were listed side by side I was again struck as to how much more qualified my opponent seemed to be. My only ace in the hole—I was a tried and true republican, active in the party, and those are the people who would be voting.

I finished up my primary campaign efforts over the weekend and on Tuesday decided there was really nothing more to be done than to go vote for myself, (don't ever let a candidate tell you they voted for the other guy—they didn't), then gather my family and head over to GOP headquarters that evening when the polls closed. As they say in the Midwest, "its all over but the shoutin." So now it was time to go and see if there would be shoutin' or cryin'.

There was shoutin'. The republicans came through with flying colors and I won the primary election. I won in nineteen out of twenty one precincts with a 485 vote margin, or fifty-eight percent victory. I won. I actually won. Our county chairman asked each of the winning candidates to come forward. Then he presented us to the crowd as the slate for the fall election. Wow—I really won. That was soooo cool.

Of course the newspapers were there—more free publicity, and lots of hearty congratulations from everyone involved—it was a real high. My opponent came over and offered me her congratulations and then I began celebrating for a very short time. I had a great time that night, but I knew that the very next day I would need to start planning my campaign for the General Election. That campaign was going to be a lot more difficult—I had a really formidable opponent.

Chapter 3
The General

My dad had told me that having a primary election would be in my favor if I won. My campaign for the nomination would give me a leg up on the Democrat candidate in the fall—he didn't have opposition, so he didn't campaign. That saved him a lot of money, time, and stress, but I think my dad was right, my primary campaign helped me gain a lot of name recognition. And it was a good thing too, because the Democrat candidate for clerk was going to be very tough to beat.

My opponent was the government and civics teacher at our local high school and had been for thirty five years. His name recognition in Plymouth, the county seat and largest community in the county, was incredible. Not only had thousands of students gone through his classroom, he knew many of their parents and families. Having been at one school for so many years, he also had many friends and colleagues that he had worked with for a very long time. Those bonds were tight and went way, way back. And, he was an incredibly nice man. Again, at least the campaign would not be ugly.

Although he had served on the Township Advisory Board, his only other government experience was out of a textbook. The study of government is very different than the actual application of government. Believe me, I wish it was as easy as the books say it is. I didn't have much government experience either, but unlike my primary opponent, I did have a clerical background and we were running for an administrative office, not a legislative office. I knew my administrative skills would serve me well as clerk, but I had a major hurdle to get over the name recognition that he had, especially in Plymouth.

On the other hand, he did not have the advantage over me out in the county, so that is where I really concentrated my efforts. In the primary, I was defeated in two of the three precincts in German Township, where my opponent was from, but it was still a Republican strong-hold, and now it was Republican against Democrat. I wanted to make sure that I got all of the Republican votes, and as many of the independent votes as I could. Plymouth was pretty evenly split at that time, between voters in the two parties, but the county almost always voted Republican. There was no doubt my party affiliation was in my favor, but it was not necessarily a given!

Even though we had six months until the general election, there was no time to sit idly by. I had made it over the first big hurdle, so I wasn't about to stop now—this was for all the marbles! I was now part of the Republican slate of candidates so there would be party help in this campaign—a welcome relief from having to do it all on our own. I also had more people come out to support me since I had won the nomination. My committee grew and a few donations (very few) came in. We were still funding most of this ourselves, but we were a bit more comfortable with the chances of it actually paying off, ie, employment at the end of the road.

We decided to continue using the same basic campaign materials we had for the primary. After all, I didn't want the voters to forget who I was, not after all that hard work. Using different materials and slogans might possibly confuse them and I certainly could not afford that so we continued with the what we had. I did have a new, professional head shot taken, but we decided to stick with the family picture. It was okay, and who wanted to put Steve (and Mom) through that again? We made a few minor changes to the brochure, such as the date of the election, etc; talked Tom's client and friend into making another batch of buttons; I had more 'where you vote' cards printed up; and of course I still had my "Leavell For Clerk" straw hat.

A couple of weeks after the primary election, there was a meeting of the Republican slate with the GOP central committee to inform us of what the party would be doing for us during the campaign. I knew that I would need to plan for parades, festivals, etc, but I wasn't sure exactly what that meant. Well, I soon found out!

Two years earlier, in 1980, the Republican candidates had used bicycles in the parades. They all rode together as one unit and it had been very popular, as well as memorable. Memorable was very necessary because the Democrats had an active party member that played in a band, and he got his band together and they rode and played on a float with the candidates. That was tough to beat in the memorable category, especially since they were pretty good players and played lots of upbeat and patriotic music. Even I would have liked to ride on their float.

Now, bicycling was very different in those days than it is now. The only people who wore helmets and protection were the folks who raced bikes. I had a bike, with a baby seat attached, and rode from time to time just for pleasure, often with one of the boys on the back. Since it had been so well received in the previous county election, we all agreed that it would be okay to do it again.

When I was young, my bike had been my main form of transportation for many years, so I am very comfortable on a bike. However, I did not have a lot of experience riding at parade speed—which is very, very slow—while trying to wave at the crowd. Also, the suggestion was made that the aforementioned baby seat should be occupied; by none other than Steve. Now, we have already established that Steve had begun his development of an incredibly independent streak, so everything with him has basically been done by negotiation. He of course thought it would be fun to ride on the back of mommy's bike—both my boys always enjoyed those bike rides—but this was not a normal ride through the neighborhood or park. This was serious. He would have to be friendly, smile, and for crying out loud he would have to be cute!! People love cute kids. When he wasn't being stubborn and contrary, Stevie was a blonde, four year-old, darling little boy, so he could really be an asset for me, if he wanted to. Time would tell.

The parade season started with the July Fourth parade in Argos, and ended with the Blueberry Festival Parade in Plymouth, on Labor Day. The party provided signs with our name and office for us to attach to our bikes and I hung mine on the basket on the front of my bike. We made arrangements for another candidate with a pickup truck to transport many of the bikes to the parade sites, so all of the details were taken care of.

On July fourth, the entire family traveled to Argos to get ready for the parade. Now, anyone who has ever been in a parade knows that unless you are the Parade Marshall at the front of the parade there is a lot of standing around, waiting for your turn to go. That is not so bad if you are basically a social person and like to visit with the other people standing around waiting to start. Steve was not. He had a very difficult time understanding why he couldn't play in the dirt until it was our time to go. It was a summer day, why did he have to stay clean?

Finally, it was our turn. I donned my obnoxious straw campaign hat, strapped Steve into the seat and set off on the parade route with my fellow candidates. As I already mentioned, we had to ride our bikes very slowly so we wouldn't crash into the unit in front of us. Not only is slow difficult, it is especially difficult with a four year-old on the back, swaying from side to side, so that he could see around me. I kept telling him to sit still. He kept telling me that he was (and he kept swaying from side to side). I finally realized that to him he was being still, since he had remained sitting, but it's all in the semantics. Four year-old boys don't understand semantics, they only understand SIT STILL. He continued to sway.

Eventually Steve and I developed a comfortable pattern, he would sway, I would lean opposite, I would wave to everyone, he would wave when he saw his dad and brother, occasionally he would sit still, and at least he never tried to climb out of the seat while we were stopped—parades always have stop time. We really became a pretty good parade team, he loved being involved, and all the spectators along the parade routes thought he was just soooo cute. Bingo.

The party central committee also prepared brochures for us. These included pictures of federal and state candidates as well as the local group. The focus was on the local candidates, so instead of just submitting a head shot photo like the federal and state folks did, we had group pictures taken. These were taken outside, in a park. It was a beautiful setting for the pictures, and the candidates were divided into groups reflecting the type of offices they were running for ie, Judicial, State representative, etc. I fell into the County administration group which consisted of two men and two women. It just so happened that two of the other candidates, a man and woman, were considerably older and the other male candidate was about my age. We were all dressed up in business clothes, the men in suits and ties, she and I in suits and heels. It was a very nice picture, but really looked much more like a family portrait than anything resembling candidates for public office. The pictures from the brochure are also what the party used for newspaper ads. They ran a series of ads with the group pictures, as well as individual ads for each of us. It was a very effective, impressive ad campaign and I was very proud to be a part of it.

Not only is the summer campaign about parades but it is also about fairs and festivals. Although there were several festivals and fairs throughout the summer, the biggest event for the campaign was the Marshall County Fair. Yes, Indiana still has the traditional 4H fair—lots of young people with their livestock, the carnival midway, good food that is bad for you, and of course the commercial building with all of the booths. Both political parties had booths at the fair and competed for the attention of the fairgoers; who you hoped were mostly from your county and could vote.

Part of the fun of the commercial building booths are the 'freebies.' Just about everyone there gave away a trinket or gimmick of some sort. They also had drawings for 'free' items, sometimes things as neat as a TV or stereo, sometimes free water or a free home inspection for bugs, or whatever they could use to draw the folks to their booth.

Well, Republicans and Democrats aren't any different. We want everyone to come to our booth, pick up our literature, register to vote if they hadn't already, and of course meet us and see what wonderful folks we were so they would know to vote for us.

I decided that the best thing to give out at the fair booth was balloons. I had balloons in all colors, that said "Leavell for Clerk." (What else?) Of course, the balloons were most popular with children, so the parents would bring their kids to the booth for a free balloon. I tied the balloons to their wrist, or stroller, or mom's purse, or whatever was available since they were blown up with helium and we didn't want any of the little ones to loose their balloons. Even so, some got loose and it wasn't long before they were flying high above the fairgrounds—all with my name on them. Not only were the balloons popular with the kids, the other candidates loved passing them out; it gave them something to do and made it easy to get the people into the booth.

We were all expected to work at least one shift at the fair, but in the interest of not missing anything, I worked every single night. It was exhausting, being on my feet and on my game for 4-5 hours every night for a week. I talked with hundreds of people, and blew up, tied and passed out hundreds of balloons. To this day I can tie a knot in a blown up balloon faster than anyone I know. It is comforting to know that certain skills were well developed during the campaign.

The summer campaign season actually was a lot of fun. Along with the parades, fairs, and festivals, we continued to go to the various fundraisers and events throughout the county. There were many other kinds of fund raisers that we attended besides fish fries. Such as spaghetti dinners (the kids' favorite); and pancake breakfasts to name a few, but probably the favorite of everyone in our family was the Culver Corn Roast.

This was a fundraising event to beat all fundraising events. They sold hamburgers, pop, and all the corn on the cob you could eat. Now, I know that many regions have food items that they are famous for, or maybe a restaurant that serves something special, but

Indiana has the best fresh corn on the cob in the entire country. Hoosiers know how to do corn!! This event was held in the city park along the shore of Lake Maxincuckee in the middle of July. You could have as many ears of corn and as many hamburgers as you wanted for something like $5.00 a person. People would be sitting around all over the park with these huge paper plates piled high with corn cobs stripped clean. We would get so full we could barely move, and then go back and get some more.

Over the years we became experts regarding the fundraising dinners throughout the county. During a non-election year (for me anyway) we didn't attend quite as many dinners but we did have our favorites on the circuit and always attended those. When you are a public official it is important to continue to support the community events, even when you're name is not on the ballot (especially when it meant lots and lots of sweet corn).

Ever since I had children in school, our family calendar ran from the first day of school to the last day of school. Even though the boys played ball, took swim lessons, went to camp, and all the other normal summer activities, it was still a relatively loose time of the year and our time was not very organized during the summer. The summer campaign season was great fun, but it as it wound down I began to get back into heavy campaign mode.

Once I began to think about school starting, I also began to think about the fall campaign. This would be much more intense than the summer had been. I did an inventory of my campaign materials to see if anything needed to be replenished. We had everything available at the festivals and fairs, but people really don't pick up much of that stuff. I was in pretty good shape, so I began to get things in order to start door to door campaigning right after Labor Day. That would give me two months to cover the county; at least the towns in the county, that is. I had given up trying to knock on rural doors. Every farm had at least one dog in the yard, and many of them are not all that friendly. I love dogs, but not dog bites, so I decided to try and contact those folks in other ways.

The party also provided fifty yards signs for each candidate. We really didn't think fifty was enough, so we were trying to decide how many of our own we wanted to buy, and if we wanted them to look the same as the party signs.

Then my husband came up with the great idea to take the left over bumper stickers and put them on each side of a 2"x 4" stake for yard signs. As it turned out, most people felt the same way we did about stickers on their cars, so although some were used by our most devoted supporters and ourselves, we still had a lot of stickers. They looked very much like the old Burma Shave signs that we used to see along the road, back in the very old days before interstates, when boomers were kids and the shaving cream signs along the state highway always had a message; some folks will remember. It is sometimes tough to determine when to put the yard signs out; kids will take them as Halloween pranks, and the weather can destroy cardboard signs in no time. However, our orange bumper sticker signs were indestructible as well as obnoxious. Not only did they hold up through the last weeks while they were out, we were able to use many of them in the next campaign.

Since the yard signs that the party provided all looked alike, except for the name of the candidate, the office they were running for, and the color, we decided that using the left over orange bumper stickers was the best way to make my signs stand out. And we were right. Not only did these signs save us money, but they were copied. A Democrat candidate for state representative used the same idea in his next election, two years later. Of course, he said that it was his idea , but we came up with it first. "Imitation is the greatest form of flattery", so they say.

The party would also run a series of newspaper ads and radio spots, so we decided to augment those with ads and spots of our own. We designed ads that told all about what a great candidate I was, how I could do the job, blah, blah, blah. All of that was fine, but the best ads we ran were during the last week of the campaign, and were nothing more than the text and design of my bumper sticker, running vertically along the outside edge of the newspaper page: LEAVELL FOR CLERK in white letters on a black background. Impossible to miss, impossible to misunderstand, and very effective.

The last 60 days of the campaign—from Labor Day to Election Day—were pretty much nonstop for all of us. I started my door-to-door campaigning again, doing most of the same things I had done for the primary. On Saturdays we met as a group, somewhere in the county, for breakfast, then split up the community and covered the streets with each other's literature. This was a nice change from going door-to-door by myself during the week, and helped me cover a lot more territory. From the very beginning I did not knock on doors on Friday evenings or Sunday. We often spent Friday evenings as family time, and I used Sunday afternoons to try and catch up at home, and maybe even rest a bit.

Along with the door-to-door campaigning, there were more speaking engagements during that fall. Candidate nights were popular with many organizations around the county, which meant complete slates from both sides were in attendance and each candidate was to speak for a couple of minutes regarding their candidacy and why they should be chosen.

I was a speech major in college so I am accustomed to, and very comfortable, speaking in front of an audience. Because of this background, I always prepared my remarks and then practiced, practiced, practiced. I was amazed at the number of candidates over the years who assumed they were good speakers and never made any effort to prepare remarks or practice them.

These folks (from both parties) often stood at the podium and rambled on and on, way past the two minutes allotted, boring everyone to death and saying absolutely nothing. I guess that's why politicians, even local ones, have the reputation for being 'windy' and not ever saying much worthwhile. That is generally true. It probably didn't matter that so many were bad speakers since most of the audience was made up of other candidates, their spouses, the committee that planned the event, the press, and a few people who wandered in from the bar to see what was going on—drink in hand.

As the days got shorter and the political season was finally coming to an end, I began to feel the exhaustion of the campaign. It is a tradition in Marshall County for the Republicans to have a campaign rally on the Sunday evening before election day. It is very well attended, and that is the final presentation of the complete slate together. It is a large family event and was very exciting for a first time candidate like me. That Sunday evening is when I officially ended my campaign for Clerk of the Court. I decided that I had done everything I possibly could, from the very beginning, and certainly since the primary in May I just wanted to stay home on Monday, rest, re-group, and have a normal evening with my family. So I did.

On Tuesday, November 2, 1982, as a final push, I went to the German Township voting place, where all three precincts voted, around 5:40 AM. I handed out campaign materials for a couple of hours then moved on to another location. I spent the entire day traveling from polling place to polling place to try and convince any last-minute, undecided voters that I was the person for the job, and trying all day not to throw up from my nerves.

At last the polls closed and we headed to GOP headquarters to watch the returns come in. When we got there, about 6:45 PM, the place was packed. My supporters came to me with sad faces—the Plymouth precincts were in and I was behind. Not by much, but definitely losing ground. The outlying precincts were not in yet, and they were predominantly Republican, so I had to keep my hopes up. That is what I told myself as I tried not to go into panic mode or cry.

I began drinking 7-Up to keep my stomach under control, and sat down to wait with everyone else. At this point, most of the other folks at headquarters stayed away from me—they don't know what to say to a loser, so they ignore you. Little by little the other precinct results started to trickle in. West Township, just west of Plymouth, I lost, North Township, just north of Plymouth, I lost. Then here came little Tippecanoe Township—I won that one, then Bourbon Township, I won both of those precincts, Polk Township came in strong for me, and all of a sudden I was maybe within reach. Then German Township—where they thought I worked so hard, because they always saw me in my obnoxious hat—came in with three big wins and I pulled ahead. Things were looking up. Then last, but certainly not least, came Union Township—home of the Culver Corn Roast—with a big enough win in those two precincts to put me over the top and with enough plurality to not worry about the absentee votes that may not have all been included.

When my friend and precinct committeeman brought in the results from Culver, and showed them to me, we both just started screaming and jumping up and down—I won. I really won! I cannot begin to describe the exhilaration, the excitement, and the astonishment that I had actually won. By this time, I was running on adrenaline and no longer needed 7-Up. I needed a beer. About that time, my husband came up to me, handed me a beer, gave me a great big hug, then disappeared into the crowd. Some things never change. My son TJ, who was 10 by then, was also very excited, and even Steve, who was almost 5, picked up on the excitement and gave me a big hug. He was sure that being my parade partner had put us over the top. No doubt.

After all of the results were in, and the new officeholder-elects had all been introduced, the crowd began to thin out. We headed for home with our very tired sons, and tried to settle ourselves down. Several of our friends came back to our house, and not long after we were home my opponent came to my door to shake my hand and offer congratulations. He had been to headquarters but I had already left, so he came to the house. It was a very classy gesture from a very classy man, and I was sometimes sorry there had to be a loser in this race, but I was very glad that it wasn't me.

On Wednesday morning, Tom and I sat over coffee and began to analyze the last 9 months; all that had happened, what we did right; what we would change in the next campaign; and last but not least, we studied the numbers. There was absolutely no doubt that I was a 'county' clerk—I did not win one single precinct in Plymouth, but I hung in there, close enough to not get too far behind. I only won the race by 365 votes, very close out of 13,011 votes cast in our race. Not close enough for a recount, but certainly not a landslide by any means.

The reality of the situation finally began to sink in. Mary Lou had a job. However, remember that this is a 'holdover' office, so I would have to wait a year before I took office. Although I was elected in November 1982, the actual beginning of the term would not start until January 1, 1984. My predecessor, Mary B Haas, ran for, and won, County Auditor, which is the other holdover office in Marshall County, during that same election. So she would actually remain as clerk for a year before she began her new job as Auditor.

On one hand, the holdover was good for me because Steve would not be starting school for another year, in the fall of 1983. On the other hand, when you work that hard to reach a goal, and you are successful, it is really hard to wait around for it to start. Fortunately, I was friends with the current Clerk, Mary B, even though she was a Democrat, so I felt pretty confident she would work with me to give me a chance to learn the job. I called her that weekend and she was very gracious. We decided that I would start in January and would work three days a week in her office as a part time employee. I would take the summer off, the last one I would have with my kids for a while, then I would work everyday in the fall, helping her conduct the city elections and learning all that I could while she was there.

Mary B and I both felt very strongly that "Republican" and "Democrat" ended at midnight on election night. From that point on, you serve all of the people as an elected official; an attitude that I carried with me during my entire sixteen years in office. That allowed us to serve all of our constituents the very best we could; and created some of the most fun times that I ever could have had with another person, surprising a great many people because of our different party affiliations. Reaching across the aisle is whole lot easier when there is some fun involved.

The next eight years, while I served as Clerk and she served as Auditor, was an incredible time for both of us. Because we were both active in our state associations we became known all around Indiana as the "Marys of Marshall County"—and what an adventure it was.

Chapter 4
The Marys of Marshall County

As I said in the previous chapter, my predecessor was Mary B Haas, the current Clerk of the Court and Auditor-elect. Mary was a Democrat, one of few elected in our county, and was extremely popular. She was one of the friendliest, kindest, most generous people I have ever met. Not to mention funny. She had an incredible sense of humor. She was a master story-teller, and most of the stories were about the unbelievable things she had said, done, or had happen to her over the years.

Mary B was a lifelong resident of Marshall County. She was raised in Bremen, a small town in the northeast corner of the county. Her husband Fred, was born and raised in Plymouth, so both of them had very deep roots. They had two children, both of whom attended Plymouth schools and were also well known. Mary's popularity as a county official was unequaled, so hers were some tough shoes to fill.

When Mary ran for Clerk in 1974 she ran against the current County Auditor. He was well known and was, of course, a Republican. Being Republican in Marshall County was a definite advantage, but not necessarily a sure thing. There were other women in some of the county offices, but not as many as men. So it was still a relatively new concept—female office holders! When Mary decided to run, she was not working as a full time teacher although she did have a degree in elementary education. Her opponent didn't know her, so he assumed nobody knew her and ran an ad in the newspaper with the line "who is this nameless, faceless woman, with no credentials, running for office" with a blank picture next to his statement. Well...that made every woman in Marshall County, including me, mad. She creamed him on election day and the very small, very significant 'woman's movement' in Marshall County began. The coolest thing about it was, instead of getting angry herself, Mary B laughed and said she just might change her name to 'nameless, faceless, woman.'

Mary and I were friends before the election so I knew there would not be a problem with the changeover. We had decided the best thing for me to do was start working for her the first of January of the holdover year. That would give me time to rest from the campaign and deal with the holidays. I would also take the summer off, except during the budget season, to spend that time with my boys. The clerk is a very demanding job and I would not have that much extra time in future summers. She also thought she might be able to train me to handle her office while she went across the street to start learning her new job as County Auditor.

I showed up for work the first week of January prepared to do whatever she needed me to do to start learning the job. I was not prepared, however, for the awkwardness of the situation with her staff. As in any supervisory job, we surround ourselves with people who are loyal to us; in this case, political loyalty. Needless to say, most of her staff were Democrats and they weren't sure what their job situation would be when the year was over. Since she was replacing a Republican Auditor there was a certain amount of 'job switching' we would be able to provide to the staff members of both offices. However, some of the jobs were really technical and it made no sense to replace those people who were already very well trained, just because of politics. Not all political people would agree with us, but from the day after the general election, November 3, politics ceased to be a factor for either one of us, except when absolutely necessary regarding political party responsibilities as officeholders.

Of course, at this point I was just a part time worker with no clout, no knowledge, and not much of a paycheck. I was in a 'we shall see' mode regarding the staff and was not about to make any decisions or statements when I was still a year out. However, it did not take me very long to figure out who could stay if they wanted and who would not be asked back; and it had only to do with work ethic and attitude—nothing to do with the way they voted.

Not long after I began working with Mary and her staff, it was time to attend a meeting conducted by the State Election Board. Since a large part of the Clerk's responsibilities was conducting elections, she was mandated to attend this meeting. There she would learn about any election law changes or updates, as well as the nuts and bolts of conducting elections. Now, Mary had been in office for seven years and conducted many elections, so it wasn't all that new to her, but it was certainly all new to me.

We traveled to Indianapolis and would be there for a two-day meeting. Since that included overnights, it was not uncommon for election vendors to set up hospitality rooms to encourage the election officials to come in, have a drink and a snack, and check out their newest products. That was the social time for the meeting and an opportunity to meet lots of the newly elected clerks.

Of course, Mary already knew many clerks because she was ending her term. She began to introduce me to many of her friends and colleagues from around the state. It didn't take very long for us to realize that most of these people were astounded that she had brought me along—I belonged to the 'other' party. That is generally not done. When an office changes parties, very rarely will the incumbent offer to train their successor. She and I simply did not work that way. It was a spirit of cooperation from the very beginning regardless of political choice.

Eight years later, I followed Mary B into the Auditor's office and the same thing occurred, although by then our colleagues and friends were used to our strong friendship and respect for one another. By this time, Mary and I were well known all around the state, because of our deep friendship, the great sense of fun that we both shared, and because we had both been very active in our respective state and district organizations throughout Indiana. Our willingness to serve our constituents in the best way we could (and that usually meant putting the political differences on a shelf in the closet) made us very unique.

Our last trip together was in December of 1991, at the County Commissioner's state meeting in Indianapolis. Once again, we shared a room, hit the hospitality rooms, laughed and talked with the vendors and other officeholders, and had a great time together. As usual, every time we entered a room the comment was made, "here come the Marys of Marshall County—Mary B and Mary Lou." They all knew this was Mary B's 'last hurrah' in county government so we shared lots of stories and laughter from her experiences over the years.

Mary B. was several years older than me, and although we were great friends, and colleagues, I will always consider her my mentor in local politics. The first thing she taught me was to "CYA—cover your ass" (a lesson learned frequently and thoroughly); to remember that you are always "on the record" until you're not; and to use my own great sense of humor as my coping mechanism, just like she did. These are lessons I continue to use everyday—they are even true in my "after county government" life.

Together Mary and I traveled many miles all over the state, she as auditor, me as clerk. We often shared hotel rooms, drank Lord knows how many gallons of beer in the hospitality rooms, sometimes laughed until we cried, and even played a little golf together. We shared secrets, friends, and screw ups. She sometimes helped me with a problem because of her experience, I sometimes helped her with a problem because of my better communication skills. We didn't always agree, but we always got along. I will never forget all that she did for me as a rookie clerk and county official with no clue what I was walking into.

After she left the auditor's office, Mary and her husband retired to Florida. They made many trips back to Indiana to visit family and friends, but we didn't always have a chance to touch base with each other. Although, on one of her visits, the county commissioners were getting ready to have a ground-breaking for a road project that started before Mary became auditor. It was completed during my first term, but I didn't have as much time invested in it as she did. When I saw her, I talked her into coming to the ground-breaking and throwing a shovel of dirt. She agreed and it was really neat to have her there with all of the principal people who had worked on the project, and to have our picture taken for the paper, with her included.

We exchanged Christmas cards for many years and tried to keep up with each other, my growing family, her growing grandsons, but like so many times, life gets in the way. Mary B was diagnosed with cancer and was very sick. When she died a few years later, I was sorry that I couldn't get back to Indiana for her service. We shared something so unique—friends and experiences together that created memories for a lifetime.

I try to always remember her grace and generosity over the years as I became the 'old clerk' and new clerks arrived on the scene. I also continued to try to help new auditors during my two terms in that office. Mary's kindness, patience, and understanding helped me become an award-winning county clerk—and hopefully a kind and generous teacher to those who came after me.

Thanks so much Mary B; for your love and laughter and friendship.

From the other Mary from Marshall County.

```
                    MANY MOONS AGO, IN 1983
            YOU BEGAN THE DIFFICULT TASK OF TEACHING ME.
            I WAS LIKE A SHADOW, ALWAYS STAYING NEAR
        TO LEARN EVERYTHING I COULD YOUR HOLDOVER YEAR.

            WE WORK SO WELL TOGETHER, MARY LOU & MARY B.,
            EVEN THOUGH YOU'RE A DEMOCRAT & I LOVE THE GOP.
            YOU SAID IT WAS A BIG JOB, BEING THE COUNTY CLERK
            AND BOY WERE YOU RIGHT, IT WAS A LOT OF WORK.

        I FOLLOW YOU AGAIN, TO THE OFFICE ACROSS THE STREET
    YOUV'E SPENT ANOTHER YEAR TEACHING ME, AND AGAIN IT'S BEEN A TREAT
            YOUR MOST IMPORTANT LESSON IS NO MATTER WHICH GUY WON,
            WE PUT ELECTIONS BEHIND US AND BE SURE THE JOB IS DONE.

            NOW AS YOU LEAVE THE COUNTY FOR YOUR FAMILY & FLORIDA SUN,
            I THANK YOU FOR MAKING THE LESSONS SO MUCH FUN.
        YOU'VE BEEN MY TEACHER, MY MENTOR, BUT MOST OF ALL MY FRIEND,
            AND IT WILL NEVER BY THE SAME FOR ME, AS YOUR TERM
                            COMES TO AN END.
```

I presented this poem to Mary B on her last day in office.

Chapter 5
The Family

When I decided to throw my hat in the ring and run for public office I was thirty-two years old. By the time I took office in January, 1984 I was 34 and one of the youngest officeholders in the state. There were only ninety-two clerks (Indiana has ninety-two counties for those who are wondering) and my husband kept telling me what an elite group I now belonged to. He thought I had accomplished quite an achievement, and I guess I did, especially when you top it off with my being so young, and it seems extremely young as I look back on it today. As I write this, both my sons and step daughter are all older than I was when I was elected to public office. Also, I am a grandmother now, which somehow seems like an even greater achievement.

One of the reasons I was able to accomplish that goal was because of the support my family gave me. My husband, Tom, was 39, my son TJ was 9, and Steve was 4. Tom was thrilled that I now had a full-time job, TJ thought it was cool that my name was in the paper a lot, plus he was beginning his lifelong passion for politics and current events, and Steve? Well, Steve just cruised along, sometimes interested, sometimes not.

Tom was a State Farm Insurance agent in Plymouth and had been in business since November of 1970. His being self-employed was a real asset in many, many ways. Not only was he available to attend many daytime campaign functions with me, he was occasionally available to watch Steve during the day, before Steve started school.

Tom only had one secretary in his office, so over the years he 'adopted' my staff as part of his own. His generosity to those gals was never ending. Many of them became his policyholders so he often stopped in at the court house laden with goodies with the State Farm logo. He provided desk calendars, regular calendars, and all the cute little squeezy stress pigs, as well as the 'beanbag' pigs that everyone displayed on their computers. He also was the funding source for sixteen years' worth of gifts to everyone for Secretary's Day, gifts to everyone for Christmas, and financing many Christmas staff parties and dinners. Of course, I could write checks on his State Farm business bank account, so he didn't always know just how generous he had been!! But my girls loved him—certainly more than they loved me.

TJ was nine years old when I ran for office. He was very interested in my campaign and was eager to help in any way he could. He asked lots of questions about the campaign; what it was all about; the differences between Republicans and Democrats (it was not so clearly defined as it is today); and anything else he could think of, which was plenty. He went with me as much as he could, depending on the event and if it was appropriate to bring a child, and when he attended those events he absorbed everything around him.

When Steve started school in the fall of 1983, I was working full time at the Court House, although I was not yet in office. He and TJ attended the Catholic school across from the court house. Since kindergarten was only half days back then, it was handy to have him nearby so I could take him to day care on my lunch hour. The following school year, when I was in office full time, and he was in school full time, he switched to the neighborhood public school and TJ moved on to the middle school.

By the time I left county government sixteen years later, they were both out of school and in the working world. But both of them, even Steve who was less interested than his brother, had a knowledge and sense of government that is very rare in young people their age at that time because of our many dinner conversations and political activities. I knew they had been very proud of their mom, the campaigns I ran, the way I conducted myself in office, and the friends I had around the state. It wasn't always easy for my family, but they hung in there with their love and support—that is all I could have asked for.

Three days after my fourth term in office ended, my husband of 30 years and 6 months died. And my life was forever changed—again.

With my first Tom, at the local paper, The Pilot-News, *when I announced my candidacy for Clerk of the Marshall Circuit Court. December, 1982*

Filing for office with Mary B (Note the nose pencil). The woman in the background was filing for a township office.

The infamous family portrait for the necessary brochure.

The front page of the necessary brochure.

The candidate photo in the county brochure that looked like a family portrait.

The obnoxious orange and black bumper sticker that nobody wanted to put on their car, so we turned into yard signs.

One of the many summer parades with me in my famliar candidate straw hat (with the obnoxious bumper sticker headband) and Steve on the back of my bike (not leaning too much).

LEAVELL

For

CLERK

 MARY LOU in '82

My 'very clever' and cheap handout for the campaign.
(We had a LOT left over... want one?)

WHERE YOU VOTE

BOURBON 1 & 2
Elementary School Gym

CENTER
1 County Buliding 1st Floor Lobby
2 Plymouth Fire Station
3 Webster School
4 Ply. High School East Entrance (across from Football Field)
5 Civil Defense Building
6 R.E.M.C. Building

GERMAN
1&2 Bremen High School
3 Lake of the Woods Fire Station

GREEN
Santa Anna Church

NORTH 1 & 2
Lapaz Elementary School

POLK
Polk Twp. Comm. Bldg.

TIPPECANOE
Tippecanoe Fire Station

UNION
1 Beach Lodge
2 New Town Hall

WALNUT
Argos Community School

WEST 1 & 2
West Elementary School

SUBJECT TO CHANGE BY COUNTY COMM.

Part 2 - Clerk of the Courts

"My father had a simple test that helps me measure my own leadership quotient: When you are out of the office, he once asked me, does your staff carry on remarkably well without you?"

—Martha Peak

Chapter 6
Learning To Be A Boss

They are "deputies" not secretaries.

Naturally, all county offices need workers; those wonderful people who come in every day and do the very difficult work of local government. Working for the county can be quite rewarding. Although the pay is usually not great, they do have wonderful benefits—full insurance, pension plans, paid vacation, and sick days. In our case, there were sixteen paid holidays for the non-essential employees, and a forty-hour work week with five hours of paid lunch time. (Jail and sheriff personnel worked 24/7) It is difficult for county councils (the fiscal body) to justify paying high wages with tax dollars, so they try to make up for the lower pay scale with added benefits. Whether or not that is fair or even financially sound is totally subjective.

In some of the offices, including clerk and auditor, the full-time staff members take the same oath as the officeholder, thereby 'deputizing' them. A deputy has the very same legal authority as their boss, including signing their name. This means that my 'deputies' could sign my name to all documents, checks, etc. The only difference is that after they signed my name, they included their initials.

When I was a young bride in the late nineteen sixties, I worked in a small, family-owned insurance agency. There were four ladies in the office, including me. I enjoyed my job there and learned a lot, but I always maintained I would never work in an office full of women again, unless I was the boss. Well, I found out that being the boss isn't that easy either.

I was fortunate over the years to have very capable, trustworthy staff working for me. In the few cases that an employee didn't work out, they moved on, or I moved them on. I didn't have to let very many people go, and only once did I hire someone who just never got it and didn't make it past the ninety day probationary period. I always felt like my service to the public was only as good as the people who worked for me and represented me, so I did my best to be loyal to them and always 'have their back.'

I am a huge advocate for women's equality and rights. I have enormous respect for the women who came before me and fought so hard for all of us, and cry for the rights that politicians today are trying to take away from women. But one of the most frustrating things I have learned over the years is the tendency for a large percentage of women to be their own worst enemies. Women tend to take things personally, hold a grudge, and sometimes get in a snit, which makes for an uncomfortable work environment. Some days it drove me nuts.

I didn't have very many rules for my staff, outside of the norm, but there were a few things that were very important to me:

- Show up and be ready to work on time.
- Dress appropriately for the job—no jeans, super tight pants, plunging necklines.
- Never, ever call and say you can't work because you have cramps—take a Midol and get to work, we all deal with that.
- Never, ever cry in public. If you are crying in public someone better be dead.
- Acknowledge every person who walks in the door as soon as you see them. If you are busy tell them you will "be right with them." Ignore no one.
- Treat everyone who walks in our door with respect, regardless of their politics, even if they are not very smart and/or smell bad. We are always kind. We treat everyone the same.

We couldn't always give the public the answer they wanted, but we could always give them good, courteous customer service.

The Clerk of the Court has a large full-time staff, all deputized. (Part-time employees were not deputized). When I started as clerk I had eight full-time deputies. Over the years, as the job expanded and the county grew, my staff also grew. In 1985 I added a deputy when I moved the County Court filings into my office. I added a full-time election deputy in 1987, as well as moving the small claims deputy into my office. In 1989, I added two full-time employees in order to film and record old records for destruction.

Although each deputy had her own responsibilities and areas of expertise, there was a lot of crossover of job duties. Everyone took, and processed, child support payments; everyone accepted new case filings; everyone prepared marriage license applications; everyone answered general inquiries; everyone did historical research on a time-available basis; and of course everyone answered the telephone.

Probably one of the hardest jobs requiring my signature was processing support checks (my support deputy signed my name all day long). I tried to get the county to let me buy a 'signature' add-on for the printer, that we could take off and lock up at night, but they wouldn't let me. They didn't think it was safe.

These were the days before debit cards and one time, my support deputy told me that she had signed my name on her own check when she was paying for groceries because she signed my name so much more frequently than she did her own. I had a grocery store clerk asked me once, after handing her my personal check, if I was really Mary Lou, because she had so many child support checks come through to be cashed with my name on it. She always wondered who I was!!

Over the years there were lots of gals who came and went in my offices. Some stayed with me almost through my entire four terms. I was able to work in the clerk's office during the holdover year and that meant I could observe Mary's staff and get to know them. It allowed me to determine who would make the transition well, and who would not. When I started as clerk, some of Mary's gals stayed in the clerk's office, and some of her gals went with her to the auditor's office. Some didn't make the transition at all, and other new people were hired on.

When term limits require officeholder changes it can be very unsettling for the staff, especially if the political party changes too. Of course, I tried not to let political affiliation be a factor, I cared way more about competence, knowledge of the job, attitude, etc, but that was not necessarily what the party 'leaders' cared about.

My opponent in the primary election was the Circuit Court Administrator and her younger sister was a deputy clerk. When I won the primary, her sister was very concerned that I would not want to keep her on my staff. It took her many months to finally get the courage to ask me what I was planning to do. I assured her that I had watched her work for those months and would very much like her to stay. The race was not personal, I liked her sister (who remained in her job with the court) and as long as she continued to do her outstanding job we would get along just fine. Unfortunately, she had many issues in other areas of her life that she was unable to cope with. This sweet, competent, attractive young lady took her own life in December before I took office in January. I know it had nothing to do with working for me, but I always felt so bad that I did not have a chance to show her that I really did want her on my staff. It was a difficult way for Mary to end her time as clerk, as well as difficult way for me to start.

After I finally took office in January, 1984, I began to slowly transition the staff to doing things 'my way.' Although, I will admit that at thirty-four years old I wasn't totally sure what 'my way' was. I had a clerical background, and was a great researcher with wonderful organizational skills, but management skills and training, not so much. It was definitely going to be 'on the job' training for me, and some of those gals knew it and tested me every day.

I had learned, and always believed, even at that young age, that the only way to be truly successful in any endeavor—marriage, family, work—was to have good communications skills. I was a speech major in college, and a pretty good writer, so I thought my communications skills were above average. I also felt that the best way to avoid miscommunication was to talk to the entire group at the same time and the only way to do that was with staff meetings. That would give me a chance to talk to everyone, and everyone a chance to discuss concerns, questions, ideas, etc with me and with each other. The problem with having staff meetings during office hours is the lack of available time. Our office was just too busy to 'stop' in the middle of the day and talk to each other. So, I asked them to come in early, before work. I provided breakfast (at my cost, no cost to the county) and gave them 'comp' time for the extra hour. It wasn't easy for those with children (including me), but they all complied and it worked out pretty well. I had originally planned to meet on a monthly basis, but that was not practical so we decided on a 'need basis.' If anyone had a general concern they came to me and I kept track until we had enough to discuss to merit the extra time. Of course, some didn't like it at all, but others were thrilled and thought it was "about damn time"—those people found the meetings quite valuable.

Over the years I have worked other places where staff meetings were held with various success. Some just went on and on and accomplished nothing; some places didn't have them at all; and some did a pretty good job. I have found though, that the organizations that have regular (not necessarily often, but regular) staff meetings tend to function better.

In the beginning, since I was a brand new officeholder with no experience, I was very dependent on my staff. Fortunately, the lady who served as Mary B's first deputy agreed to stay. However, I couldn't make her my first deputy because she was a Democrat. (Stupid, stupid, stupid, but political patronage was firmly in place and I couldn't change it, I could only work around it). A large part of this lady's job was overseeing judgments handed down from the courts. When a monetary judgment is ordered by the court, we recorded it in the judgment book and the money could not be sent out until it was 'released' by the attorney.

For example, we had a call one day from a litigant asking when he would receive payment. I checked the judgment book and saw that the order had been entered, I checked the Trust register and made sure the money had been paid, so I cut the check and put it in the mail. Well...big mistake! A few days later the attorney came in, looked at the book, saw the money had been released, and was livid; he was supposed to be paid from that money and then the balance could be released. I had sent the money without a release, something we never, ever were supposed to do. The very experienced judgment deputy who was supposed to oversee the book (and did not know that I had sent the money) suggested that I call the bank and see if the check had cleared. It had not, and I was able to stop payment on the original check, write another check to the attorney, and pay the balance to the recipient. The attorney was still a bit miffed, (not very gracious to the 'new' girl) but satisfied and a new check was written to the litigant. Lesson learned—one of many. Not only was that very-experienced deputy going to save my butt on many more occasions in the first year, she was also a kind and delightful woman to work with. I will be eternally grateful for her knowledge, patience, and sense of humor as she 'trained' me to be the clerk.

Generally the gals got along pretty well with each other, especially when you consider the close quarters we worked in, the absolute total lack of privacy, and the stress of a really busy office. Although I inherited some staff, from time to time I did have to hire people. Of course, these were public jobs, so it was necessary to advertise all employment opportunities, but people were usually hired by recommendation. When I had an opening for a full-time position I always offered it to part-time employees first. Not all of them wanted to work full-time, but some did. And of course, there was always the call from a political person who 'had a friend' and wanted to know if I had any openings. It should be noted that I was not the one who determined how many deputies I would have. That decision, along with the salary, was made by the County Council. But I did decide who would fill the slots that were already in the salary ordinance. Some of my hires over the years were really spot on, others, not so much.

I had one young lady who was recommended by another county officeholder. She was a good deputy in that she did great work, was on time, etc. But she tended to struggle with her co-workers. It would seem that when someone wasn't around she would tell the others 'stories' about the absent co-worker—often stories that would get them in trouble. When I would ask about the problem, I would be told that it "never happened." Eventually, I would bring them both together, make them sit down, and tell me the story in front of the other person. Invariably it would turn out that the story wasn't true and apologies were made. I finally told her that was enough, and if she couldn't get along with her co-workers she would have to move on. Then the problems stopped.

She was a very young single mom and still had a lot of growing up to do. Most of the ladies in the office were older and married, so chit chat about spouses was not uncommon. I'm not sure why that bothered this young lady, but all of a sudden flowers started being delivered to the office for her. Of course, everyone wondered who this very generous guy was and when would we get to meet him? She constantly deferred, and we all thought it was very unusual that he never came to the office. Her ex-husband did from time to time but no boyfriend. Eventually she admitted that it bothered her that she wasn't married so she was sending the flowers to herself so we would think there was a man in her life. Good grief, who cared. But as I said, she was very young. Eventually she decided to move to a different state with her daughter and start a new life. I wished her well, and figured when she grew up she would be a crackerjack employee for someone or some company.

I hired another lady who was probably one of the most competent, capable, intelligent deputies I had ever worked with. And boy, was she funny. She came to work for me even though she didn't need the job, because she needed something to do. She had sons the same ages as mine and they were all in school. Plus, her husband traveled a great deal for his work so she decided to get a job to fill her days. It was supposed to be part-time, but eventually she worked full-time. Her husband was thrilled. He said her working full-time saved him about thirty-six thousand dollars a year—her pay plus what she would not be spending because she was at work and couldn't go shopping. Not only did she do a great job for me and the county, she was an absolute stitch and the fact that she didn't need the job (the money) probably gave her a lot more confidence to just say what was on her mind.

One thing that was consistent in my office was, when a new person started, the first time one of their children called the office, they always asked to speak to "my mom." We had many moms, which one did they want. Of course, after that they would ask for their mom by name, as did husbands, friends, etc. Except one. One gal's husband always asked for Mrs. _____. Well, their last name happened to be the very word that my funny lady's husband called an erection, so when Mrs. funny lady answered the phone for the first time and the caller asked for Mrs. _____ she was laughing so hard she could not continue and just hung up. Poor man had to call back. Then there was the time she came stomping into the back room and took off her dress (nobody around but co-workers). When I asked why she was undressing she told me she had her dress on backward. When I asked her why she had her dress on backward she said, "Well I had to beat three kids this morning before I left for work, I was stressed." (She didn't really beat her children.) Another day, it was unusually quiet in the front office when a delivery of a dozen roses was made. It was the wedding anniversary of another deputy and her husband had sent the flowers.

Funny lady took one look at the bouquet and said, "Well when you get a dozen roses, that is worth at least a bj"—needless to say I was very, very glad the office was empty of customers because we were all ROFLAO! I never knew what would come out of her mouth, but I always knew that I never had to worry about the quality of her work.

It was not uncommon for attorneys to make a mistake when they filed their paperwork for various cases. One time an attorney came in with a file that was in error and she waited on him. When it became evident that the error was from his office, not ours, he very indignantly asked, "Well who is going to fix this?" She answered, "Well, you are", and then turned around and went back to her desk. He meekly gathered up his papers and went back to his office. We loved it. Eventually her husband was transferred so she took her tremendous skills, work ethic, and incredible humor to another state. Our office was never quite the same without her.

Although Indiana was a right to work state, the county had implemented a ninety-day probation period for new employees. The commissioners were always trying to get the elected officials and department heads to document any employee problems so that when, or if, you had to let someone go, there wouldn't be a lot of repercussions that the county would have to deal with in court. Unfortunately, not many bosses documented like they should, but the probationary period was very helpful. I had hired a lady one year who came with great qualifications, experience, and recommendations. As it was, she really, really worked hard. But as her probationary period was coming to an end, my first deputy came to me and asked me not to keep her. I was quite surprised because I thought she had been doing a great job. The answer was yes, she did work hard, and was cordial and nice to work with, but the problem was she never accomplished anything. She spent the entire day moving papers around on her desk and looking very busy, but never actually got any work done. Turns out, she never really understood the job and was too embarrassed to ask for help, so it was one big vicious circle. I think she was disappointed and relieved all at the same time. I saw her around town from time to time after she left my office and she was always very friendly, she never held a grudge against me for letting her go.

That however, was not necessarily the norm. I had hired another lady who was also highly recommended and very competent. She did a great job overall, although she was a bit of a gossip and I had to remind her that what happened in our office might be public record, but it was not up to us to be the town criers! One day her son was visiting and came into the office to see her. I didn't really have any problem with that, we all had families and children who were welcome in the office anytime. When he got there she took her coffee break and they both went into the break room to visit. Unfortunately, after her break when she went back out to her desk he followed her, pulled up a chair next to her desk, and continued the conversation. I probably would not have noticed, but they were laughing and talking very loudly, and disturbing her co-workers. I kept thinking he would wrap it up and leave, but as the afternoon wore on it became obvious that was not going to happen. Eventually I went over to her desk, reminded her that her son was always welcome, but he would have to leave now because they were making too much noise and she had work to do. He very graciously got up and left, but I could tell she was quite angry. The day ended and she went home, but I thought about it for a long time, because I wasn't very happy with her attitude. The next day when she came to work I called her into my office and reminded her that if she was going to work for me she would have to follow my rules. I thought that was pretty reasonable, but she did not. She tossed her resignation letter on my desk, said "I already have decided," and walked out. I was okay with that, but I felt bad because she and her husband had been my husband's long time policyholders and she also canceled her insurance. (She must have felt bad too because years later when my husband died she brought a huge tray of shrimp cocktail to my house.)

However, the best employee in the world does you no good if she doesn't show up for work. I had one deputy who really struggled with attendance. She worked a vital desk, child support, an area that must always be covered. If she wasn't there, then someone else had to stop what they were doing, get up from their desk, go to the support desk and handle the payment or whatever. In an ordinary day, no one minded helping—everyone has to leave their desk from time to time, for lunch, nature calls, whatever. But she would often start complaining on Thursday afternoon that her head hurt, or she had a stomach ache, or something else was wrong. Then I would hear the comments and complaints, everyone knew she was going to call in sick on Friday, the busiest support day of the week. After a while I got really tired of it, so I pulled her into my office and told her that absenteeism was causing too many problems in the office. She needed to go to the doctor and find out what was going on, and in the meantime, if she wasn't going to be at work she would have to move to a different job in the office, one that didn't require constant coverage. I knew she wouldn't do that, it was a cut in pay. But, she got the idea and her absences declined measurably.

I think the biggest mistake I ever made as an employer was thinking someone was irreplaceable. This support deputy had been hired by Mary B and was in charge of automating the support desk. Back in those days we couldn't buy software, it was all custom written, so getting the records into the system and having the system do what you want consistently was a great challenge. There were many problems, rewrites, hours of lost work, etc. The system would go down and she would have to go back and start hand typing the day's checks, then integrate the two systems, hand-written and computer-generated, into the record. Not easy and incredibly frustrating. By the time I took over, the software was working pretty well, with just a few blips. But I will give her credit, she hung in there and made it happen.

Indiana participated in a federal program wherein a person could file for support payments through the state welfare office if their ex spouse was very far behind. Most participants were single mothers who struggled financially and this was a program to help them get the money they were entitled to. Then, when and if their ex-spouse made a support payment, his record was credited and the money was paid back to the state. Part of the funding that was paid back came from tax refunds that were intercepted by the federal government and the money then applied to the back support. This program required us to do some extra work on behalf of the prosecutor's office, so that they could process and prosecute delinquent support payers, and on behalf of the clerk's office that received and disbursed the funds and needed to keep the records up to date. The county was paid for participating in this program (like they had a choice) with the funds sent to the county to be split in thirds: one third to the prosecutor, one third to the clerk: and one third to the county general fund. The funds, which were referred to as IV-D funds, were not absorbed into the regular budgets of the prosecutor and clerk. Instead they were allowed to use the money any way they wanted, without approval of the county council. As you can imagine, this caused some conflict between these elected officials all over the state. The county council did not like any officeholder being able to spend money that they did not appropriate, and the commissioners did not like any officeholder spending money without their permission. Now, I never used my IV-D funds for anything outside of the office, in fact I didn't use the money much at all, except for the big ticket items, my mezzanine and the new furniture when we moved to the new courts building. But I can't speak to clerks and prosecutors around the state except to say that I only heard of a few instances of misuse—very few.

Part of the record keeping in the clerk's office was to keep track of tax refunds that were 'intercepted' by the federal government and state. These funds were sent to the state as reimbursements, but needed to be recorded in the delinquent payers' record. These were federal funds that were paid through the welfare office in Indianapolis. One day I received a phone call from a woman who said she was our representative from the state office and would I be available for a meeting in Plymouth, along with my support deputy, the prosecutor and his support clerk, and the county auditor. I said sure, thinking it was about administrative changes, or whatever.

Well, you can imagine my surprise when we get to the meeting and I find out that my support deputy has not been processing these tax intercept records in a timely manner, if at all. Now, I had, on a regular basis, asked her about it because I knew it was important to be in compliance with the program. Not only for our own funding, but the payers deserved to have their records updated if they were not getting their tax refunds. My deputy looked at everyone in the room and admitted that she had not been honest with me when she had assured me she was up to date. I was absolutely floored and humiliated. The lady from the state told me that if we didn't get the records caught up in a certain amount of time she was going to withhold the payments to the county for everyone. Why should the other people be penalized when they did nothing wrong? I also asked her why she had not brought this to my attention sooner so I could have fixed it instead of waiting for several months, and she just said she had been in a car accident and had been out of the office recuperating. She assured me that was the way it was going to be, so I had better fix it. End of discussion.

When the meeting was over, both the prosecutor and the auditor (Mary B) told me not to get too upset, just catch up and everything would be fine. I think they felt like the lady from the state blindsided me. However, when my deputy and I got back to the office, I should have told her to get me the records, clean out her desk and leave—she had lied to me. But I wasn't confident enough that I could get someone else in there, and I was so angry I could hardly say anything at all. She followed me into my office and apologized over and over. I gave her a week to get caught up and if she had to work over, so be it, she was not going to get comp time (we did not have overtime) for the extra hours. She did work hard and got it all caught up, and continued in that position for the rest of my term, but I never really trusted her again.

Probably the most disturbing and distressing situation I encountered regarding staff was watching the abuse of some of my staff who remained after I left the clerk's office. I had only gone across the street, and like all companies, public or private, word gets out. My successor in the clerk's office was a Democrat and a male. Neither of those things meant two hoots to me, I tried to offer him the same training and help that Mary B had given me. However, he had been a supervisor at his previous job and there is a definite difference between managing women and managing men. I tried to make him understand that women take things more personally than men do, and he would have to earn the respect and loyalty of the people who were already in place—in other words, not his hires. He needed those folks and their expertise, so it was to his advantage to keep them and treat them right.

When I hired someone for my staff, my main criteria was: could they do the job and do it well. Sometimes I missed the mark and it didn't always work out. When I did hire someone, what I looked at was their ability, experience, attitude, etc. Attributes that made them a good employee. I was aware of the politics involved—everyone always wanted you to hire strictly from the party—but I only paid attention to that in regards to election workers. I didn't ask or pay any attention to a prospective employee's personal life; that was simply not my business, as long as they did their job and did it well.

One of my deputies had hired on during my first term at the recommendation of another deputy. We had sons of comparable age and I knew her through the ballpark. She was a Navy veteran and an incredibly hard worker. Eventually she ended up helping with the traffic desk and when we moved to the new office I put her there permanently. She worked with my first deputy, and when I left for the auditor's office, my first deputy went with me, so I thought my successor would put her in charge of the traffic desk. He moved a current deputy into that slot, but that person had no experience with that particular job. Unfortunately, my successor did not consider the same qualifications for employment that I did and decided he didn't want my traffic deputy to work for him because she was gay. He would never admit that, of course, but he worked very hard to get rid of her. He and her co-worker in traffic concocted a silly story about her trying to break into the co-worker's home on a Friday night. Now, that was just ridiculous and everyone knew it. But he thought that would be enough to get her fired, so he suspended her without pay. The county attorney went ballistic and said, "No, you can suspend her, but you have to pay her." Well, he wasn't about to pay her for doing nothing so he moved her to a job filming old records in the basement. It was a huge waste of resources, nobody else knew the traffic desk like she did, and she was bored out of her mind. However, she decided to appeal his decision—that made him mad so he fired her. I was delighted, (for me, not for her) because by that time I had an opening in the auditor's office for a settlement deputy. Settlement is an extremely difficult job and she was one of the few I knew who was capable of doing that job. In the meantime, she hired an out-of-town attorney and sued the county for unfair firing. She eventually won her case and settled with the county's insurance company, at the encouragement of the attorney. I think he knew the county would get killed if the case went to court and this seemed the better solution. Good for her. She continued to work for me as my settlement deputy for the remainder of my two terms in office, and for another two auditors before she retired.

Another incident involving one of my former deputies and my successor happened when he just up and fired one of the gals who worked in the basement filming old records. She had been doing that for a long time, since the inception of that department. He maintained that she was sleeping at her desk during the afternoons, which was poppycock. Everyone knew he didn't like her husband, so he fired her. Well, she fought back too, hired a local attorney, and asked for a hearing in front of the commissioners. I was part of the hearing because I had to take notes (I don't think he expected me to be there) and I was astounded at the way he and her co-worker from the basement lied. Her co-worker didn't like me because I had gotten on her about her tardiness and told her if she couldn't get to work on time she couldn't continue to work for me. She gave me some excuse about getting her kids to school, I reminded her we all had kids to get to school, and the rest of the staff made it to work on time. It was not negotiable. So, during the hearing she said that my former deputy had a pillow in her drawer and took it out and put it on her desk so she could nap. Well, that was about the dumbest thing I had ever heard, but since she said it under oath the commissioners believed her and the other the deputy did not get her job back. What a crock.

I am a true believer that what goes around comes around and it was proven at the next election for clerk and auditor. There were no candidate filings to run against either of us for the primary election, so it was up to the county chairmen of each party to fill the vacancies. If they did not, then we would each be unopposed for re-election. Well, the clerk, in his stupid way of trying to 'orchestrate' things, convinced his deputy who lied about my traffic deputy, to file a form to allow the county chairman to nominate her as a candidate for auditor. Well, he failed to realize that I still had some friends who worked there and one of them called and told me at 11:00 am (with a noon deadline) that I now had a race. When one of my deputies in the auditor's office heard that, she said, "Then I'm going to run against him!" She had been my small claims deputy in the clerk's office and was familiar with the office. She ran down our county chairman just as he was walking into the clerk's office to fill the vacancies he had. She stopped him, signed her name, and he filed her candidacy and now we both had opposition. Guess who won. My successor manipulated himself right out of a job, and it never had to happen if he would have just left well enough alone. Needless to say, when my former deputy took office as clerk, she did not keep the liar on the staff, so they were both out of work.

Sweet.

Chapter 7
I Do, I Do, I Do

As in most states, there is only one place to get a marriage license in any given county, and in Indiana that place is the clerk's office. But the clerk's office is only open from 8:00 AM to 4:00 PM weekdays. Since those hours don't accommodate many working people, and they can't go shopping for another clerk's office with better hours, my predecessor kept the office open until 6:00 PM on Tuesday evenings. Her deputies took turns staying late and she stayed with them to help if they got busy. I liked the idea, so I continued those hours. However, it was not uncommon for me to receive calls asking if I might consider meeting a couple on a weekend, or after work during the week. Generally they had a very good reason, so of course I was happy to help.

I always found it charming when couples came into the courthouse to get their license because usually that is the time that the whole thing was beginning to be 'real.' The license was only good for ninety days, so they couldn't really apply too far in advance. They were often excited, nervous, and just generally giddy. One young man was so excited that, as he was leaving the office after I personally had done the license, he said, "Will you marry me?" I was a bit startled, so I told him I would love to, but I already had a husband and didn't think he would want to share—the kid was really was cute, though!

Although the clerk's office was officially closed on election days, we were already there to conduct the election, so it was not uncommon to have people come in to get their marriage license, forgetting it was election day, We tried to accommodate them if we were not too busy, but always helped the young Amish couples who came in from the other side of the county, because frequently they had paid someone to drive them to the courthouse and I didn't have the heart to turn them away.

There are age limits in most states regarding when a young couple can marry and Indiana was one of those states. At that time, you had to be eighteen years of age to get married without permission. At seventeen you needed a parent's signature, at sixteen you needed a judge's permission and proof of pregnancy, and marriage was prohibited for anyone fifteen or younger.

A minor thing like age didn't stop some people and it was always a difficult situation, so when those folks came in, my staff just automatically called me to handle it. If they had all the proper paperwork and it was in order, then I would proceed to issue a license. But sometimes, even with the paperwork, there were problems; like if one parent forbade the kids to get married, but the other parent said okay. That was always fun, getting caught in the middle of family feuds. Or the time a young couple came in to get their license, with everything in order, or so we thought. However, after they left with license in hand, we received a call from her sister stating that the prospective bride had forged her birth certificate and was not old enough. She needed a parent's signature. I chased down those kids and told them if they did not come back to the courthouse with that license, I would press charges and have them arrested. They came back, with mom in tow, and she finally signed for them, "Since they wanted it bad enough to lie for it." Go figure.

There was one other occasion when a couple who want to get married was very, very young. The parents didn't want them to, especially the mother of the bride, and it was getting very tense. Finally, the youngsters met with the judge and he ordered me to give them a license. Later, he told me that the young man was going into the service and the young lady came from a bad home, so military life might be the very best thing for both of them. They were a sweet young couple and I think he was right.

When I started working part time for Mary B in January of 1983, I learned that the clerk of the court had the legal right to solemnize marriages. Now, I never thought of myself as the 'Marryin' Sam' type of person, (if you don't know who that is, Google Lil' Abner) but it wasn't long until I fell right into that role.

I soon learned that it was relatively common, for the clerk, or any of her deputies to perform marriages. She had a few printed ceremonies that we could pick from and we tried to determine what would be the best for the happy couple. I performed a few of the weddings during my holdover year, but Mary and the regular staff did most of them. However, it wasn't long after I took office that the wedding bells started ringing in earnest and I married lots and lots of couples—two hundred and fifty two couples to be exact—over my eight years as clerk. I still have the book with their names and the dates of their marriage. All of them.

Some of the highlights of weddings that I performed:

- Three in my home
- Three in the jail
- One in an airplane, flying over the county
- One using an interpreter for sign language because the bride was deaf
- One where the bride was Polish and did not speak English
- One request in the middle of the night—she and the groom were drunk—I said no
- One under threat of death—the mother did not want her daughter to marry
- One couple that I worried about—I wasn't sure they were capable of knowing what they were doing
- Too many to count out in front of the courthouse by the war memorial
- Several in private homes—twice to sisters at two different times—same house
- One near Halloween, at a 'haunted house', we were all in costume, me as a witch
- One couple—for the second time to each other. They didn't make it, then decided to give it another try
- Several in various event halls around town
- A few in churches

Let me elaborate:

Three in my home... One day in early February during my first year in office, about 5:00 PM I received a call while I was still at the courthouse. I was the only one there, so of course I answered the phone (no caller ID then), it could have been my family. It wasn't. This nice lady asked me if I performed marriages and I told her yes, sometimes. She asked if I might marry her and her fiance, they had their marriage license but it was about to expire and they didn't want to have to get another one. I said sure, when would she like to schedule it. She said, "Tonight." Oh. Well. I was not about to have strangers come to the courthouse when I was there alone at night, so I suggested they just come to my house in a couple of hours. They agreed. Then I decided I should call my husband and tell him what was happening. Fortunately he agreed (a good thing since they were already on their way), then my older son asked if we could do it in front of the fireplace, because it would be more romantic, especially if we had a fire. I said sure start a fire, but mostly make sure the place is cleaned up so it looks good when they get there. He did start the fire, but he did not think to open the flue, so by the time I got home the place was full of smoke, the doors were all open, and it was freezing in there. Well, the bride and groom showed up, with their attendants and their license, and we proceeded with the ceremony. They were good sports about the smoke, and my young children watching curiously. After they were married, there were hugs all around, and they were on their way. I don't remember if the house was cleaned up or not.

I did two more marriages at our house, both on Saturdays, and after the third one my husband suggested we find an old bathtub and set up a grotto in our back yard if we were going to do this on a regular basis. I did not do any more weddings at my home.

In the jail... On three different occasions I was asked to come to the jail to marry an inmate. They already had their licenses when, on all three occasions, the groom was arrested and incarcerated. I don't remember a lot of the details as to why they were in jail, but I do remember it was kind of awkward to marry a couple and then walk out of the building with the bride, but without the groom. I don't believe the sheriff ever let them consummate their marriage.

In an airplane... I had a friend whose fiance was a pilot. He had a small plane, single engine something or another (I am not an airplane aficionado,) and he thought it would be neat if they could get married while in the air. I figured, why not, and met them at the airport on a lovely, sunny, summer afternoon. And yes, my entire family came with me to see this spectacle. My husband took pictures of me, taken from the back, bent over, getting into the plane—not a pretty sight, those pictures have subsequently been discarded. There were four seats: bride, groom, one attendant, and me. I reminded the groom/pilot that he should probably stay over Marshall County as much as possible to make sure it was legal (it was, I could marry anywhere in the state), but mostly because I wanted it to be a short trip. Anyone who has ever flown in a small plane like that knows they are incredibly loud. I went through the ceremony, they repeated their vows—I think—and then we landed. We were subsequently invited over to their house for a steak fry that evening to celebrate the marriage with their families, which was nice, considering I'm still not sure whether or not they said all the right stuff—but the paperwork was completed properly so they were legally hitched.

Using sign language... This was a rather unique situation for me. The couple came to the courthouse and brought an ASL interpreter. The bride was a lovely young lady, with a gorgeous smile. beautiful blond hair, and blue eyes. She was very sweet and I could see why he was so in love with her. However, again, I can't be sure all the vows were said correctly since I do not sign and have no idea what she said, but the paperwork was completed properly so they, also, were legally hitched. And the groom seemed satisfied while they went merrily on their way as newlyweds.

The Polish wedding... This was a tough one for me, because she was very young and he was very, very old. She did not speak English and his English was not very good. I was uneasy about this marriage because I had a feeling she was marrying him to stay in this country—she was not a citizen. And I was afraid he was marrying her to have someone to take care of him. She was another sweet young bride, and it just broke my heart that she tied herself to such an old man. But, who knows, maybe they were in love. However, since she couldn't speak English, I once again had no idea what vows she said. But the paperwork was completed properly so, like the others, they were legally hitched.

Request received in the middle of the night... They were drunk, I said no. However, I did know her, she worked in the prosecutor's office. I asked her if she was drunk, she said, "Maybe a little." I told her the answer's still no and I would see her Monday. On Monday she gave me hell. Later she proceeded to marry the guy, had a baby, and moved out of town. At least I made sure she knew what she was doing.

Under threat of death... I was quietly working in my office one afternoon when one of my deputies came in and asked me to come to the front counter. That generally means there is a fire to put out, so I'd better hustle. Well, this time it was an irate mother who was yelling and carrying on, and said if anyone in our office gave her underage daughter a marriage license she would come back with a gun. (This was many years before it became common for people to show up at public places and start shooting.) I explained to her that if her daughter was underage, we were not legally allowed to issue a license. Without the parent's approval, the license would require a court order. That seemed to settle her down and she went on her way. However, at the same time. and unbeknownst to me, a deputy had just finished a telephone conversation, telling a young couple that their age would require a parent's signature or a court order for them to obtain a marriage license. Guess which couple that was.

The next thing I know, they have made an appointment with the judge and are coming in to see him. I told the judge that the mother had made some threats, so we might want to tread carefully. Well, the kids showed up for their appointment, but so did the mother. Apparently the young lady's parents were divorced and her father was okay with the marriage but the mother was not. She had threatened the father if he gave permission. He was a coward and said okay, and it landed in my lap. Nice. As it turned out, we all met with the judge, the bride and groom, the irate mother, and me. Eventually, the judge decided it was okay for the kids to get married. He told me later it was to get the bride out of the volatile situation—do you think? He signed a court order for me to issue the marriage license. None of my staff would touch it—they did not want to be shot—so I sat down at the typewriter and did my duty. When we were finished and the young man was paying for the license, they casually asked me to marry them. I about fainted. The court order to issue the license wouldn't protect me from the mother if I performed the ceremony, but I felt bad for them so I said sure, and we set a date. After it was set up, I asked the Sheriff to wander over and hang out for a little while that afternoon, just in case the crazy mother did indeed come back with her gun. He agreed, and then promptly forgot. I flew through that ceremony as fast as I could with one eye on the paper and one eye on the door in case she came in and we had to duck! Remember, this was the time before metal detectors and security at the door. Thanks, Sheriff. The mother was nowhere to be seen, so I guess the judge scared her. Thanks, Judge.

The one I worried about... There were many funny, heartwarming stories about the various weddings and marriages we performed. Actually, my deputies did a lot more of them than I did. But I do take marriage very seriously, and was quite concerned when this young couple showed up to get married. They were old enough and had come in to get their license. The three-day waiting period was no longer law, so when the license was completed and issued they asked if I would marry them. I said yes, but it just didn't feel right. They were of age, yes, but they were not ready. Neither one of them seemed to have any idea what was happening or why. I think there might have been some disability issues, but I'm not trained for that, so I can't say for sure. It was just an instinct with me, but I performed the ceremony and wished them well. I can only hope they understood what was happening and had a happy life together.

Out by the War Memorial... Like many public buildings there is a lovely war memorial on the courthouse lawn that lists the names of the Marshall County soldiers who have died in the line of duty. There are benches and landscaping around it, lots of gorgeous shade, it is very nice. I wish I could say it is a peaceful spot, but it is very close to the street. That particular street is the main east/west corridor in our little city of Plymouth, and a north/south street runs between the county building and the courthouse. Very, very busy area and intersection. I understand wanting to get married there, especially for veterans or military personnel, but because of the traffic, it is sometimes hard to hear, not to mention all the cars going by, seeing what was happening and honking their horns, presumably in a spirit of good wishes. So again, each time I performed a ceremony there, I had to hope they said all the right stuff, but the paperwork was completed properly so they were legally hitched. As you have probably figured by now, marriage is about the paperwork, not the vows.

In private homes... being invited into someone's home to perform a wedding is indeed a privilege. Often times however, their home was out in the country. Marshall County is primarily a rural county, so finding my way was not always easy. Again, before the days of GPS, I would worry myself to death that I would not find the house and ruin their special day. However, as far as I know, I made it to the homes of all who asked, and generally, after the ceremony, I was invited for cake, or whatever was served. I married two sisters, at two different ceremonies, in different years, at their parent's home and that was very special. Both times they set up a nice place in their back yard and, after the ceremony they had a big hog roast and party. My husband and I were invited to stay for the party for both sisters for both years and it was great fun.

One day I had an older couple (probably younger than I am now) come in and ask if I would marry them. They were both widowed and were planning to go visit their grown children in Florida. They were very uncomfortable going into those homes and sharing a room without being married because they didn't think it was a good example for the grandchildren. They told me that they preferred a church wedding, but they had visited several churches in the area and not one of them would perform the ceremony until they had taken 'marriage' classes. How absurd to be so inflexible. I figured that those two people, both of whom had long term marriages before their respective spouses died, could teach the classes on how to have and maintain a happy marriage. I was pleased and honored to perform the ceremony for them—two widowed, lonely people who found each other and planned to make a new life together. There is nothing but good about that.

<u>The Halloween Wedding</u>... It was becoming very common for non-profits in the area to sponsor 'haunted houses' for Halloween as a fund raiser. They would find an old home that nobody lived in and decorate it all up to be spooky and scary. Then the members sold tickets to go through the house and it was usually a very popular event for kids. One small town at the southern edge of the county, Argos, had a very active Jaycee organization at that time. Like most organizations there are members who like certain projects and in this case a young couple had made the haunted house project their 'baby.' They had worked on the project since it began. When they decided to get married, they thought it would be a grand idea if they could do in 'their' haunted house. So they called me. I was intrigued by the idea, but wasn't sure about having people walk through during the ceremony. They assured me that they wanted

the ceremony before the doors opened to the public, so there would be plenty of time. I agreed and we made arrangements. Then, as an after thought, they informed me they would be in costume, would I consider a costume also? Well, after a moment of stunned silence, I told her that I had a pretty neat witches costume from a previous year, but I wasn't sure it would be appropriate. She assured me it would be most appropriate and they would love it. So, I put on my witches costume (sans the green makeup) and headed to Argos on a Friday night to marry what turned out to be Frankenstein and his zombie bride. They had their close friends and family there, all in costume, and had called the paper. They thought it would be great publicity for their fund raiser. It turned out to be great fun actually, and we made the front page of the local paper. Pretty cool.

Various event halls... These weddings were often held at The American Legion, the VFW (called the "Hall of Heroes" by my veteran friends), and sometimes at the Eagles lodge. One thing they all had in common was a combination wedding and reception. As soon as the guests arrived, they almost always tapped the keg, opened the bar, got a beer, drink, etc. Also, there was very little coordination among the wedding wardrobe requirements. It was not uncommon to have the bride in a lovely gown and the groom in slacks and sports shirt, or some of the guests all dressed to the nines and other guests in jeans.

I had a very nice ceremony that I used for weddings, but it was very short. I could deliver it in about four minutes—with feeling. Sometimes I could have them shedding sentimental tears in less than two minutes. This was a civil ceremony, so there rarely was any praying during these weddings. However, once in a while they would ask if they could add something, maybe a reading or a song. Of course they could, what's another minute, right?

There were never any 'rehearsals' at these types of weddings, so I often found out about the 'extras' when I arrived. One time, the couple told me that they were having a very good friend sing, and where in the ceremony they wanted me to stop, turn and give him a signal to start the song. During the course of this pre-ceremony discussion, there were many interruptions, so they somehow forgot to tell me that the singer was blind. When the time came, I turned, and kept motioning for him to start, but nothing happened. Finally the groom explained the situation, so I gently touched the musician's shoulder and he began. I can't tell you what I was wearing that day, but I can tell you that my face was very, very red and sweat was running down my back until that man starting singing. As soon as we were finished, I joined the reception, a cold beer was in order. Whew.

A couple of churches... My least favorite venue for a wedding, when I officiated, was at a church. First of all, most church weddings that I have attended over the years are conducted by the pastor of that church. I am not a pastor. I am not a pastor of any church, anywhere. In fact, at that time I was a practicing Catholic. I was very uncomfortable performing a civil ceremony in someone else's church—it should have been the pastor. However, I did it a couple of times, usually because it mattered so much to the parents. Nobody ever told me why the pastors of the various churches didn't solemnize the marriage instead of me, but they didn't.

For a portion of my first term as clerk, when a couple applied for their marriage license, they had to wait three days before they could pick it up. I received many, many frantic calls from distraught grooms on Friday evenings and Saturday mornings because they had forgotten to pick up their license. Fortunately, I didn't live far from the courthouse, so I would jump in the car and run up to the office to get them their license. I made lifetime friends in doing so. Eventually the state dropped the three-day waiting period, so couples could take their license with them after they completed the application. It really made things much more convenient for everyone involved, but I never really minded putting out those teeny, tiny Saturday morning fires and saving a lot of grooms from being in big trouble. It wasn't all that uncommon for couples who lived out of town to struggle to find a time to come to Plymouth to apply for their licenses. With some regularity I would meet a couple on a Saturday to prepare marriage license when they would come to town to work on their wedding arrangements. I felt like it was the least I could do for them for something so special. Besides, it made their parents—who lived in Marshall County and could vote—very happy.

Of course, not all marriages make it, and not all of the ones I officiated did either. Although I have a record of every couple I married, I don't have a record of how many of them are still married. Many of them moved away from the county, but not all of them. And every once in a while I would see someone who I married and they always remembered me, even if I didn't remember them. That was a special time in their lives even for the ones that didn't take, and they loved that I was a part of it. I loved it too.

Chapter 8
Elections: The Nine Month Process—Without the Baby

When I started in the clerk's office, Mary B compared the election process to having a baby—candidates filed for office in February and a final winner was declared in November, nine months later. Right? Except on the final day—election day or birth day—having a baby is a lot easier. I had two babies and administered seven elections, trust me, I know. After the babies were born I got to stay in the hospital and be taken care of for a few days, sharing the limelight with my new son, everyone happy and glowing, and receiving lots of presents. After election day, not so much. The very next day I had to be right back in the office; not all of the people were happy and glowing, and I received a lot of grief! I had to start the certification process, answer hundreds of questions about why we did things the way we did (Indiana election law was not an acceptable answer to unhappy people), convince folks that nobody cheated, and try to begin catching up on all of the judicial work I had set aside to concentrate on the last few weeks of the election cycle. Yeah, having the baby was easier.

Indiana statutes dictate that the Clerk of the Court is automatically a county's election director. It is part of the constitutional duties. The clerk is also a voting member, as well as secretary, to the County Election Board, who 'turns into' the County Canvassing Board on election night when it is time to count the ballots. The County Election Board is made up of a Democrat, appointed by the Democrat County Chairman; a Republican, appointed by the Republican County Chairman; and the clerk, again, by virtue of the office. It is the County Election Board's responsibility to administer the election, carry out all of the duties of the election, and handle all election disputes. Forgive me if I whine—my fellow election board members were good guys, but they were very much part-time so guess who did all the work—Mary Lou and her staff.

Speaking of staff, when I began my first term as clerk, my election help was all part-time, with full-time hours. Elections were held in three out of the four years of my term; the presidential, the off-year, and the local elections. The thinking was that if you weren't running an election you didn't need election help. I think that was understandable in the old days, however, as time progressed and Marshall County grew it became obvious this was not the case. The election staff was working as many hours as the regular staff and didn't get any of the benefits. This really came home to me after the 1984 Presidential election.

A huge part of the election duties in those days was administering the voter registration. It was a pretty constant job to process new registrations, address changes, canceled voters, etc, so I had someone there nearly everyday. The first person I hired to work elections ended up working for me for my entire sixteen years in office. She started as part-time election, then when I moved the traffic desk upstairs into my office, she took over that job. She went with me to the Auditor's office where she served as my first deputy, and handled all of the payroll and human resources. She also performed all of the computer backups (a huge, time-consuming job in those days, until the county hired a Technology Manager).

She had been active in Republican politics, and was just scary smart, so it was not at all difficult to train her. Plus, she would take the time to look up the election statutes on her own and was not totally dependent on me, which was a rare trait. I only had a couple of other gals who would do that. She was also one of the most pragmatic people I have ever known in my life, and that came in very handy when dealing with candidates, voters, and election workers.

My first election was the 1984 primary. It was a presidential year, so that meant a great deal of increased voter registration activity. As the deadlines neared to end registration, we had a steady stream of folks into the office to register to vote, check their registration, and get information about the election. Although all of my deputies registered people as they came in, my election deputy processed all of the registrations, entered them in the computer, typed the voter ID cards, and sent them out, processed any that came back, and recorded any cancellations or changes we received regarding voter registration. In the meantime I took care of the candidate filings, ballot preparations, worked with the election workers, and prepared and handled absentee applications.

My organizational skills really came in handy during election years, to keep it all straight (while I continued with all of my regular clerk duties). At that time we had twenty-one precincts, so I purchased twenty-one, stacking, plastic trays to use for each precinct. Then, as absentee applications, worker lists, and other items came in, they were put in the appropriate tray and we didn't have to spend time 'sorting.' It turned out to be an invaluable tool and later when we moved, I had a permanent shelf built with 'cubicles' just for that reason. As the election day got closer, it was necessary for me to hire another part-time person to help. Her husband was active in

Elections: The Nine Month Process—Without The Baby

the party and she wanted to get involved. Unfortunately, I didn't realize that she never quite understood that all things were divided by, and defined by, precinct. As we completed various steps of the process we would put everything in piles by precinct. The voter registration books, the election day materials, eventually the absentee ballots, etc. On the Saturday morning before the election, each precinct inspector would come to the court house to pick up their supplies and get sworn in. So, on the Friday before the election, we would fill the canvas bags they used to carry all of the supplies. I had sent my regular election deputy out to help with the traveling absentee board, so I asked the newer gal to please fill the canvas bags with all of the supplies; again, they were in piles according to precinct, she did.

The next morning, all of the inspectors showed up, got their bags, and off they went, I didn't expect to see or hear from any of the them until election day. Well I was wrong. I was at home that Saturday afternoon when I received a phone call that one of my inspectors (they were all republicans like me) said that she had been looking through the bag and the stuff in there was for a different precinct than hers. WHAT??? Oh Boy, this was a problem. So I called a few of the inspectors I knew particularly well and asked them to check their bags. Turned out many of them had the wrong supplies. I realized right then—the gal that filled the bags didn't pay any attention to the precinct names stenciled on the bag. She just grabbed a bag and threw the stuff in it. I called everyone of the my inspectors that afternoon and determined which ones had the wrong supplies. Then I called my election board members and told them what happened, and on Monday they spent the entire day running around the county collecting supplies from one precinct and taking them to the correct precinct. We also had some other last minute, day-before-the-election-duties, so needless to say, they were not happy campers.

It is important to remember that my predecessor was a Democrat, so when it was time for the absentee voter board to set up in the hallway of the court house for walk-in absentee voting, the Democrat member of the board was very unhappy. She was a 'died in the wool' Demmie and was not happy that a Republican had won. Her husband was the Democrat member of the County Election Board and he was fine to work with; but his wife, not so much. She was very critical of everything I did that was different, and I did a lot of things different. She was absolutely furious over the mix-up with the supplies and determined right then and there that I was the most incompetent clerk she had ever worked with. I thought that was a bit of a stretch, given that was the only major mistake that was made, and we caught it and made it right, but she loved that I (through my staff) had screwed up.

I did feel better on the day after the election when the two fellows on the election board both told me, separately, that they thought I had done a great job with my first election, even with the supply screw up, and was smart enough to learn for the future. I appreciated their comments a great deal. I also realized that I would need to have someone better to help with the general election that fall, we would not have time to fix another major screw up. So I told the extra lady that I would no longer need her help. Even though I had given her a chance, she and her husband hated me until the day I left office—both offices.

One of the best things that I learned as an elected official, especially in conducting elections, was how to meet deadlines. There are not many things we do that are so deadline driven as the election process: last day to register; first day for candidate filing; last day for candidate filing; specific dates for campaign finance reporting; first day to vote absentee; last day to vote absentee; last day to certify candidates to the state; first day registration starts again after the election; just to name a few. One year, after I had hired a full-time election deputy, we were preparing the supply bags for the Saturday morning pickups. It had been a very busy day, and we were scrambling to get the job completed. I will never forget my deputy saying to me, "Well, I have to meet my husband for dinner at 5:00, what happens if we are not finished?" I just looked at her and said, "Well, we stay and finish. You will have to change your plans. We don't have the luxury of telling folks we aren't ready for election day, ours will be Wednesday instead of Tuesday, we didn't get it done." She got my point. We did get the job done that day and she made it to dinner with her hubby. However, she never forgot the lesson—deadlines are not negotiable. And if I learned nothing else in all my years in county government—you get it done and you get it done on time. For sixteen years I was faced with deadlines, not only in elections and judicial matters, but also in budgeting, financial reporting, advertising, settlement, etc. There is very little wiggle room and some pretty stiff penalties for missing the date.

Administering the elections is one of the most visible, and sometimes controversial, responsibilities of the clerk. First of all, everyone thinks they are an election expert. Often, someone would ask me a question and before I could give them an answer, they answered the question themselves—usually wrong. When I corrected them, and cited Indiana election law, they always said, "That is not right," according to their brother-in-law, sister, neighbor, aunt, father, co-worker, child, husband, wife, whatever. Everyone is an election expert—except they're not.

I had a special book that came with the Indiana law books (again, before the internet we had books) that had all of Title 3 (Indiana election law). It was a paperback manual and I had it tabbed, marked, highlighted—everything you could think of to easily find my answers. I used that book a million times a day during an election cycle. One year, the Democrat county chairman came in and asked me a question. I told him I wasn't sure, but he could find it in Title 3, he was a lawyer, he had law books. He said to me "No, you look it up, you know that stuff way better than me." Nice complement coming from the leader of the opposite party. During my last year as clerk, while administering the city elections, my deputy stuck her head in the door to ask me a question. I was looking up something for the election and she said, "Don't you have that book memorized by now?" I wish, but the Indiana legislators insisted on getting involved and were forever 'tweaking' perfectly good election laws. They should have left well enough alone in my opinion.

I have often said that one thing my years as a county official did for me was to hone my organizational and decision making skills. Nothing did that better than planning an election. I have always had good communication skills and now was the time to put them to the test. Everything had to be ready: candidate packets (with forms and instructions) before filing started; lists of voting precincts (in case one had to be changed, we needed time to find a new place and inform the public); lots of information out to the press regarding all of the pertinent election dates, etc.

Each stage of the process required its own 'plan ahead.'

First Come the Candidates:

When someone is a candidate for the first time, they are always overwhelmed when they receive their candidate packet with their financial forms. I was no different. We all hear stories in the news about candidate and campaign finances, how much candidates spend, if they file properly, or whatever. But local candidates forget that those stories are about candidates running for state and federal offices, and they are dealing with millions of dollars. That kind of funding is not generally necessary for county races, so when they see they are expected to fill out a form about their money they just panic. I did too, until I got home, took it out of the packet and looked at it and studied it. Well, it wasn't that big of a deal at all.

One year, a fellow came in to file his candidacy for County Commissioner on the Democrat ticket. He was very concerned about the financial forms and I assured him he would be fine. Apparently I did not assure him very well, because a week or so later he came back into the office and put a giant grocery bag on the counter. It was full of unpopped popcorn. Turns out he had heard that popcorn is a food group for me, I love it, and he was a farmer who grew popcorn for Orville Redenbacher, (right up the road from us in Valparaiso, IN)

Now, I was well aware that, as an elected official, taking bribes is a no no—but yes, I could be bought with popcorn and told him to come in when the forms were due, bring his campaign income and expenses, and I would show him how to fill out his forms. Actually, I filled out the form, he signed it. Whatever.

One thing the local press did on a regular basis, was come to the clerk's office and check out the financial forms filed by the candidates. They then reported on the income and expenses of each candidate, even if there were none. They also listed in the paper anyone who failed to file their report on time. Now, as part of the candidate packets, I always included a paper with all of the financial filing deadlines—in great big bold print!! But of course, when people were listed in the paper for not filing, they came in and blamed me for telling the press. (Candidate financial forms are public record, I couldn't keep them from the press.) Why couldn't they just read the simple piece of paper I had given them. The one with the filing deadlines.

Poll Workers, Please:

In Indiana, the poll workers are 'appointed' by their respective political party county chair. Each precinct requires an inspector, two judges, two clerks, and two sheriffs—one from each party. The party of the inspector is determined by the number of votes cast in the county for the previous secretary of state's race. In our case, the GOP secretary of state candidate won, so the inspector was a Republican, and the Republican candidates were listed first on the ballot, in alphabetical order. It varied from county to county, depending on which secretary of state candidate won in any given county; and would only change, maybe, every four years when the office of secretary of state was on the ballot.

The inspector is in charge of the precinct, making sure the election runs smoothly and if there are any questions or concerns it was usually the inspector who called back to the courthouse for information. The judges help the inspector in any way needed. The clerks do the necessary paperwork regarding checking in the voters, making sure they are registered, etc. The sheriffs' job is to primarily keep order at the precinct; make sure that candidates or their representatives do not get too close; keep all of the campaign materials out of the precinct; etc. For the most part, everyone was generally pretty helpful during my years, and did whatever was needed.

Because these people were paid so little, and even the regular workers only worked once or twice a year, training was very important. Mary B had always scheduled two training sessions, one in the afternoon and one in the evening. Workers could choose whichever one they wanted. We had twenty-eight precincts with seven workers in each. (When I started as clerk there were twenty-one precincts, but we added seven more at the end of my first term).

That makes for a rather large crowd at training sessions so I changed it to four sessions, two in the afternoon and two in the evening. Because the job responsibilities were different, the inspectors and judges were invited to one, and the clerks and sheriffs were invited to the other one. This made it easier to plan the training and prepare the materials. They still had a choice, afternoon or evening, but we did it on two different days. To make sure they showed up for training, they would be docked twenty dollars from their already paltry pay if they were absent without being excused. I excused very, very few workers over the years—they had to have very, very good reasons.

The polls open in Indiana at 6:00 AM, so the workers are expected to be there by 5:00 AM to get everything set up and ready. The inspectors picked up their precinct supplies on the Saturday proceeding the election and were sworn in. Inspectors swear in the other workers on election morning. Nothing is more frustrating than to receive a call the night before, or early in the morning of an election, hearing that someone can't work, so I had the county chairmen add an alternate to the list of workers for me to call. If that person knew they were going to work in advance, they were expected to come to the training, if not, then they were excused.

Occasionally, a precinct worker would work outside of their own precinct in which case they would vote absentee. Or, if they were called at the last minute, then they were able to go to their own precinct to vote, and then show up for work. I didn't have to use alternates very often, but boy was it nice to have them already on call.

After the county chairmen submitted their list of workers (and often after much nagging and prodding of both parties) I sent each worker a personal letter thanking them for their willingness to serve; telling them about their job responsibilities; explaining the pay and how it would work; and informing them of their training day.

As far as I am concerned, the precinct (or poll) workers are the backbone of the free election system in our country. They were not perfect. Some 'older' workers fought valiantly against change with the age old statement, "We never did it that way before"; some just didn't listen during training; and some were a bit more concerned with the political aspect of voting than the actual 'right to vote.' But for the most part, they were all hard-working, caring citizens who wanted to do their best for their county. All these years later, I still think so. I appreciate and applaud them.

Ballot Prep:

Over the last few years, there has been lots and lots of press and controversy, as well as lawsuits, regarding the 'gerrymandering' of U.S. congressional districts. However, that same gerrymandering also goes on in state legislative districts as well, which can make ballot preparation real tricky. Because not all state legislative candidates are on every ballot in the county, it can be very confusing to the 'uninformed' local candidate running for the first time. Sometimes they are quite upset when they don't see their name on a ballot, then I would usually just point out, "You're looking at the wrong ballot," and proceed to explain how it works.

Believe me when I tell you that I would sweat bullets over ballot preparation. I checked and rechecked my candidates, district boundaries, etc. I made sure that candidates filed their name exactly the way they wanted it printed on the ballot—if their name was James but they go by Jack, they had to tell me or it would be James. Also, they had to print their name legibly if they wanted to be sure it was spelled correctly on the ballot. I refused to be hung out to dry if I couldn't read someone's handwriting. Before I ever sent the ballots to the printer, I called the other election board members and we worked together to proof all of the ballots. Mary Lou was not going down alone if there was an incorrect ballot, trust me.

Although preparing for elections is a huge part of the clerk's job, another aspect of that job was even bigger—voter registration. The federal 'Motor Voter' law, which allows voter registration at various locations throughout the county, did not go into affect until 1993, the year I left the clerk's office, so before that, I was in charge of all of the voter registration efforts in the county. If someone wanted to register voters outside of the clerk's office, at fairs or festivals, voter registration drives, etc, they had to be appointed by their county chairman and sworn in by the clerk. We put together voter registration packets with all of the supplies they would need, a list of deadlines for everything, and general information about the election.

All of the registration cards were numbered, so I knew exactly who had what cards. That became important because every once in a while someone would fail to turn in their kit, which means the people they registered would not be put on the voter rolls—this also means that those people would not get to vote. New voters did not like that. We tried and tried to get the deputy registrars to tell the people to be on the lookout for their voter ID card and if it didn't come in a timely manner to call the clerk's office. Some registrars did, some registrars didn't.

For the most part this process worked pretty well over the years. Almost all candidates wanted to register voters, hoping those new voters would remember them and vote for them. When the registration cards were turned in, we typed up the personal voter ID card and sent it to the address on the registration. If the card came back undeliverable, we filed them away and pulled the name off the list. On occasion the registrar would make a mistake, or the post office would screw up and not get the card delivered—and the voter would be very upset on election day when they couldn't vote. They would come in to the office in a fury—then when I would pull the undelivered card they backed off. Generally.

Keeping the voter rolls up to date was a never-ending task. We made all of the changes that came in with the deputy registrar kits; changes made in person at the clerk's office; or changes that came in the mail. As long as there was a signature, we could make the change. Of course, today you can do all that online, but I worked in the dark ages when pen and paper were really important.

We also purged the voter rolls monthly, based on information from the local health department that listed the deaths in the county. If someone died outside of the county it was incumbent on a friend or family member to let us know. Some did, some forgot. Every two years we were required by state law to purge all voters who had not voted at least once in the previous two years. We sent them cards explaining that if they wanted to remain on the voter rolls, they must sign and return the card to the clerk's office. If the card came back undeliverable, then we assumed they had moved and we purged them. You can imagine, knowing people's tendency to not read and pay attention, that many of those cards were thrown away as junk mail, even though the voter still lived there and still wanted to be registered. We kept copies of every card we sent, so when the complaints came in on election day, we had our proof—but boy, these were not happy people. There is a segment of the voting population that chooses to only vote in presidential elections. This means that every two years their name would come up to be purged. I don't understand why every eligible voter doesn't vote in every single election they are eligible to vote in, but they don't and it is their choice. The consequence of their choice is that they are removed from the voter rolls, but the folks who vote regularly very rarely have problems.

One of the toughest parts of election day were all of the people who showed up to vote in either a new or old precinct, but had not bothered to change their address at the clerk's office. The law at that time required you to change your address if you moved to a new precinct, even if you did not move out of the county. Now, I personally thought that law was too stringent and if you forgot to change your address you should be able to legally go back to your old precinct and vote, change your address on the form, and make sure it was updated for the next election. I think maybe the law eventually changed to allow that, but during my terms it did not. I have said a million times, the oath of office I swore stated that I would follow all of the laws of the state, not just the ones I thought were sensible. So I had no choice but to deny their requests to vote. Of course, I'm not stupid enough to be unaware that many of them did go back to their old precincts and vote. But as long as I didn't know—so be it.

I was always amazed at the variety of excuses people used when they found out they could not vote because they had not changed their address:

- 'But the records were changed in the county tax office'—that is nice, but that is a separate office in a separate building, we don't have access.
- 'It is changed in the phone book, you could have looked it up'—not something my staff (one person) has time to do with 25,000 voter registration records.
- 'I don't care what the law says, and if I don't get to vote, I am coming to that office and shoot whoever tells me no'—okay everyone, when he shows up, you better duck, but he is not going to vote (he never showed up).

Of course there were times when we made the mistake, and when that happened I tried to graciously apologize, issue a certificate of error, and let them vote. One day I received a call from a precinct inspector telling me that a man's name was not on the list, but should be. So I did the research and told her that we had him listed as deceased and removed him from the rolls. She turned around, told him he was dead and then I heard him say, "Really, but I feel pretty good." When he came into the office to get it straightened out, he explained that he was 'the third' of a 'senior' and a 'junior' and that the 'senior' had recently passed away. He had a cute little boy in his arms and I asked his name—the voter laughed and said, "Oh, he is the fourth." Okay then.

Finally, the clock would read 6:00 PM, the polls closed (except the few that still had people in line), and we all sat down to take a breather. There was still lots of work to be done that evening, but fighting with the unhappy voters was over. Now I just had to prepare for the unhappy candidates—you know, the ones who lost.

After I left the clerk's office, the county purchased new electronic voting machines. That made canvassing (counting the votes) on election night so much more efficient. But during my tenure, we were using the old lever voting machines and paper ballots for the absentees. Canvassing is done at the polls, and we would have to wait at the courthouse until the precinct officials were finished counting their votes, finished having their dinner, and finished their paperwork (it is the government after all, there is always paperwork). Then the inspector and the Democrat judge were required to return the supplies to the court house with the ballots counted and the tally sheets ready. Then our second wave of duties would begin.

As each precinct reported back to the courthouse, we checked in their supplies, then pulled the canvassing sheets and gave them to the ever-present press reporters. Generally, they reported the results as unofficial because there rarely was a change in the tallies. However, we would not certify the final count until all the precincts were in, or sometimes the next day. Then we put the precinct bags in the election board room and began to tally our canvassing sheets.

It sounds like a simple procedure and it really was, except that the precincts didn't necessarily come in that quickly. Some of them might be having trouble with a voting machine, then the machine mechanics (who were also the election board members and canvassing board members) would have to go to the precinct and check out the problem, which slowed everything down. I swear that during my first year in office, the last precinct to come in was at least three hours behind the previous one. I was sure they had gone down to the corner bar to have a beer before they began their tally; but they swore they had not. Since I couldn't leave until everyone reported in and all of the work was completed, that first year I left the courthouse at 3:00 AM on Wednesday. I had been there for twenty-three straight hours—long, long day.

I was back at my desk by 9:00 AM the next morning. Whew. That was the longest election day I ever had, but I never got home from any countywide election until at least 11:00 PM.

The most time consuming aspect of precinct tallying was counting the absentee ballots. There were three methods of absentee voting at that time: in person at the clerk's office; through the mail (snail mail); and with the traveling board that went to nursing homes, the hospital, or private homes when a voter or voters could not get to the polls in person. We also used paper ballots for curbside voting at the precincts on election day. All of our precincts were handicapped accessible, but some folks still couldn't easily get inside, so we took the ballots to their car.

Absentee ballots include a security envelope. Then, when someone voted absentee, they placed their completed ballot in the security envelope with their name, home precinct, and any other pertinent information. When received in the election office, these envelopes were processed to be sent to the proper precinct. The voter put the ballot in the security envelope when they were finished voting—that is how they maintained their privacy. On election day, when the ballots were processed, the precinct officials were to open the envelope and immediately put the ballot in a locked ballot box, without unfolding it. They used the envelope to 'vote someone'—in other words, to mark the records that the person had voted. If it was a primary election, the record was marked R or D, and for a general election the record was marked with an X. Then the locked ballot box would be opened after the polls closed. That was how the privacy of the ballot was maintained, because all of those ballots were mixed together in the locked ballot box. There was always some debate about working with the absentees before the polls closed, but I maintained (and could find nothing to prove me wrong) that the ballots could be marked as voted during the day, but not counted. That was generally up to the poll workers themselves as to how they wanted to handle the absentees.

I do remember that during my first election, I received a call from the Democrat county chairman concerned that one of the precincts was opening absentees during the day and counting them. So, I called the precinct and checked it out. No, they said they were only marking them as voted. The inspector also told me that they didn't do anything until everyone agreed—all of the Republicans and all of the Democrats. Well, obviously someone disagreed, because they made a phone call that caused lots of trouble, and I told them to stop whatever they were doing until after 6:00. Later that evening, when the inspector brought the supplies in he asked me who had called. When I told him, he was very angry, because the fellow had agreed with everyone. It didn't bother me that someone had a concern about something happening at the precinct, what concerned me, was he didn't call the clerk's office to find out, he called his party chairman to 'tattle' on his fellow precinct workers. I made sure that man never worked the polls again—not because he was a Democrat, but because he could not be trusted. His word was just no good.

Nothing strikes fear in the heart of an election administrator more than the word 'RECOUNT.' And it was very obvious to me when I went home to bed after the 1986 election, that this was exactly what was going to happen—a recount in our county sheriff's race, and a recount in our congressional district race. Oh boy, this was not going to be easy.

The previous 1984 election had been my first election to administer on my own, and President Reagan was on the ballot. In my very Republican county, that made him a most popular candidate and the turnout was quite heavy. I learned a lot from that election, but I was really going to be tested this time!

1986 was an 'off year' election, meaning that no presidential race was on the ballot. However, we still had many important races (including my re-election as clerk) so it would not be a piece of cake. None of them are.

We had a very popular congressman at that time, Jack Hiler from LaPorte, Indiana. (He went to the same high school as our current Chief Justice on the Supreme Court, John Roberts). Congressman Hiler was a very popular Republican. He was deeply interested in his constituents and spent a great deal of time in the district. He was opposed by an attorney from Knox, Indiana, Tom Ward. Mr. Ward was pretty well known around the district because he had practiced law in many of the surrounding counties. It was a very tough race.

We also had a very close race for sheriff. Our Republican sheriff was running for re-election against a popular Democrat who had been sheriff during a previous term-limit cycle. Both were well-known, both were well-respected, and both were experienced law enforcement officers. Both had campaigned hard, so this was also a very tough race.

That evening, as the election results began to trickle into the clerk's office, it became quite evident that both of these races were very close. Since Marshall County leaned Republican, Congressman Hiler was doing okay, locally. However, the regional news media indicated that the race was tight elsewhere. The sheriff's race, on the other hand, kept going back and forth between the two candidates. The lead would switch back and forth as each new precinct came in.

At the end of the evening, when all of the precincts had returned their supplies, forms, and ballots, it looked like Sheriff Tyson had lost and his challenger had won. However, because it was so late, and because we hadn't yet had an opportunity to go through the paperwork submitted by the precincts, I suggested that we not certify the results that night, but instead, come back in the morning after everyone was rested. The canvassing board (which is also the election board) agreed. I notified the press that we would be meeting in the morning and would certify the election results after we checked the paperwork.

The next morning I started getting things prepared for the canvassing board. The supplies are returned in large canvas bags so we had to 'dump' them out on the floor. We removed the books with the voter records so my staff could begin marking them, then we took out the paperwork that we would need to check the counts. We had decided to only check the results of the two tight races, sheriff and congressman, there were no other close ones. This would save us a great deal of time. All the other materials, including the ballots, were put back in the bags and put away in a secured storage.

I decided that the paperwork we needed to check included the voting machine tally sheets, the absentee tally sheets, and the 'blue sheets' that certified the absentees for each precinct. When the precinct officials open up the back of the voting machine, they record the number of votes for each candidate on the tally sheets. Meanwhile, the count for the absentee ballots for each race is written on another tally sheet. Then the absentee numbers are transferred to the voting machine tally sheet and the two are totaled. That is the final count per candidate. We made sure that the number of absentee ballots certified by the election board matched the numbers listed on the tally sheet. If the numbers did not match, then we had to review all of the ballots, including the 'spoiled' ballots (the ones not counted because they were marked in error and set aside). Our job was not finished until all of the numbers matched.

In the case of this particular election, all of the tally sheets were filled out correctly, except one. In one small precinct, Congressman Hiler had received nine absentee votes that had not been transferred to the machine tally sheet—an easy clerical error to make in the late hours of a very long day. When they were added, his total vote increased by nine. That was the only error we found in all the precincts in all of the races. As for the sheriff's race mentioned earlier, it should be noted that we found no changes at all. Our results showed the challenger, Mr. Sime, winning by eight votes.

We all three agreed to these results—the Republican canvassing board member, the Democrat canvassing board member, and me. I was a canvassing board member by virtue of my office. Remember, all of this was done in front of the local press. No one was hiding anything. We signed the final canvassing sheets and then I began my process of certifying the results to the Secretary of State.

However, all of us knew that there would be a recount filed in the sheriff's race. Any candidate in a race that close would have done the same. The law requires a recount commission to be appointed by a judge, so it would take a little while for it to fall into place. A few days later, Mr. Ward filed for a recount in the third congressional district between he and Congressman Hiler. That recount commission would be appointed by the Secretary of State. Oh boy, this was going to be real sticky.

The Saturday morning after the election I received a telephone call from an Indiana State Police officer. He told me that he had been ordered to meet me at the court house to gather all of the election materials and secure them until the state recount commission could meet. He also told me that the press would be there. Now, I had been working nonstop for many weeks on the election, so I had not done much around my house. My husband was gone for the day attending a Notre Dame football game and my kids were off with friends. I decided to get busy and clean my house that had not been touched for weeks so that the health department would not come and take my children. In other words, I was a mess. When he said the press, I thought he just meant were the two local newspaper guys who covered everything. Imagine my surprise when I arrived at the court house and, lo and behold, here were all the regional TV stations; lights on, cameras on, reporters dressed to the nines, and Mary Lou in her cleaning clothes. I about died. Later that evening when the coverage hit the local news my phone started ringing and boy, did my so called 'friends' ever rag on me about wearing my Chicago Bears sweatshirt (I was still a fan then) and jeans to the court house. Everyone knew that I was always professionally dressed when I went to work—and I was on TV in jeans and a sweat shirt. I was mortified.

Elections: The Nine Month Process—Without The Baby

After the election materials were secured by the state police, I had no access to them. The paper materials, including my personal notes, were locked in the election office in the county building and the lock on the door was changed. The lock on the door to the building that housed the voting machines was also changed. The keys to those locks were kept at the state police headquarters. Nobody was going in that office, nobody, for any reason. That meant I couldn't do any of my post election work, give out any information to anyone, water the plants (they all died), nothing, It was incredibly frustrating.

Finally, several weeks later, all the rules, regulations, and logistics were worked out so we could have our recounts. Both of them at the same time. Auditors from State Board of Accounts handled the congressional recount and the local recount commission handled the sheriff's recount. The bi-partisan local commission agreed that, in the case of the absentee ballots, voter intent would be the only basis for changes. State law is pretty specific about those ballots. They are to be marked a certain way, no extra marks, etc. And the precinct officials followed those laws. However, the recount commission decided that voter intent was the criteria—if you could determine the intent, then the ballot was counted. Adding the few ballots that had been set aside throughout the county, the results of the election changed, and lo and behold it ended in a tie. A tie. For county sheriff. The Democrat county chairman was in the room during the process, and when he saw the result he immediately looked up the law (he is an attorney) on how candidate ties were settled. When he threw the law book across the room, I knew it was not good for his side. Indiana election law states that in the case of a tie, the deciding votes are cast by the county fiscal body—the County Council. All seven Republican members of the Marshall County Council. Well, everyone in the room knew who would walk away with that victory.

Personally, I think that is a terrible way to handle a tie. It means that seven people in Marshall County were allowed to vote twice. However, it is the law, and they followed the law, so of course we certified Sheriff Tyson as the winner, and I swore him in for his second term. To this day, I still think it should have been a special election. That would have cost a lot of money, and it would have meant incredible extra work for me and my staff, but it would have been the right thing to do. However, that is not the law, and we followed the law.

At last, the 1986 election was finally over. We knew who our sheriff would be and we knew who our congressman would be. Everything was back to normal and I could finally begin the post election work I was waiting to do, and oh goody, I could get started on preparation for the 1987 municipal elections.

Wait a minute—not so fast—the sheriff's race and controversy was far from over. It just got worse, and what should have been stopped by the Democrat member of the county election board, was perpetrated by rumor, innuendo, and lack of communication—you name it. In his effort to make it look like the Republicans cheated, he didn't realize if we went down, he was going down with us. He was there for every official action and he signed every piece of paper. When I reminded him of this fact, all the color drained from his face. Things were going to get pretty ugly.

As I write about my election administrator experiences, I can't help but feel some resentment toward all of the misinformation, misunderstanding, bad communication, and just plain lying that caused me to be accused of something I would never have dreamed of doing in my life—cheating on an election. I would never have done that and I have never met any other election official during or after my term in office who would have done it either.

Elections: The Nine Month Process—Without The Baby

One day as I was returning from lunch, I saw a cameraman from the CBS television affiliate in South Bend outside the courthouse interviewing a local attorney. When I asked my staff what was going on they said, "He is talking about you." Me? Why would they be talking about me? Well, it seems the local attorney, who was also the Democrat county chairman, (the same man who threw the law book across the room after the sheriff's recount) had filed a complaint with the Secretary of State's office that he "had reason to believe the sheriff's race was fraudulent." So, five months after the fact, the Democrat election board member and the Democrat county chairman arbitrarily decided somebody cheated, probably me. I was stunned. Election record keeping is very complex and trying to cheat would require extensive skills and huge amounts of time. I had neither, nor a willingness to do such a thing.

What I couldn't understand is why neither of them came to me with their concerns before they made these very serious public charges. I lived and worked in a rural area. Plymouth is a small town. I knew these guys. Their kids went to school with my kids. The news reporter's son was an altar boy with my son, for crying out loud. What were they doing?

Eventually the facts came out that a former Republican County Commissioner had allegedly overheard a telephone conversation between two other Republicans, "...it's okay. Tyson *[the sheriff]* is taken care of, he will win." Also, someone had stopped by the election office right after the election and had seen me talking with the Republican county chairman. That person was convinced that we were changing votes because nobody else was in the office.

So, on another sunny Saturday, this time in May, 1987, five months after the recounts were over and done, I get another telephone call from another state police officer. He said he would be at my house to pick me up (he was also a personal friend) to go to the election office to lock up the election records. Again. Of course, I asked, "Why," but he didn't have much information for me, just that he had orders from the Secretary of State.

Well, since this was way out of the norm, I started making phone calls. I couldn't get in touch with any of my judges, so I started calling attorneys. I finally found one at home who was willing to accompany me to the office to see what this was all about. The officer came to my house in his squad car, so needless to say it was quite disturbing for my children watching me leave in a police car. Now granted, I was riding 'shotgun,' not in the backseat cage, and certainly no handcuffs, lights, or sirens, but nevertheless—mom left in a state police car. Not a cool thing to watch.

When we got to the election office, the state police officer told me again that he had orders from the Secretary of State to pick up all of the election materials until an investigation could be done. Well, that was all well and good, but there was no written order. Now, I knew and liked this young officer, as did my attorney, but no paperwork? No compliance! In retrospect, I realize I should have left right then and there and told them to call me when they got their paperwork in order. But they said they would contact Evan Bayh, Secretary of State, a particular officeholder I despised because of the way he handled the congressional recount, and get their order. I said, "Fine, we'll wait, but nobody is getting anything I'm responsible for without something in writing." So we sat and sat and sat, and waited, and waited and waited—almost five hours. Both my attorney and I had family members at home waiting for us, so we were just about to say, "Enough, come back on Monday," when another officer showed up with the order. I'm still not sure it was valid, but I was tired, my attorney was tired, and we all wanted to go home. So they loaded up my election materials and hauled them off to the state police post.

Needless to say, the press had a field day with this petition. They printed the accusations in the papers and talked about it on TV and everyone began to wonder if maybe there was something to it. I consistently told everyone I talked to that I had no idea what the charges were about, there was nothing wrong with the elections, and I was sure the investigation would prove me right.

And it did.

A special prosecutor from another county was named. The investigators had determined that, if there was anything to this, it would be found in altered absentee ballots, or ballots cast after the deadline. They checked all of the paper trails, talked with almost every single absentee voter that they could contact (over two dozen), interviewed every other party named in the complaint, and eventually determined that this election was clean as a whistle. It was proven that the fellow who allegedly overheard the telephone call was totally confused and there was no call at all, and what someone thought they saw in the election office was the county chairman writing down the certified election results from the canvassing sheets. We were just chatting. They finally admitted they didn't really see any evidence of ballot tampering, nor even any ballots themselves. There was nothing fraudulent about any of it and the cost to the county was $1900, on top of all of the normal election expenses—just to verify what I had already told every single person involved.

Later, much later, after many, many articles in newspapers around the state, reporting that there was absolutely no fraud in the Marshall County election, the Democrat county chairman called and asked to take me to lunch. I wasn't really interested, but I was curious about what he wanted. Turns out he wanted to apologize for the accusations he made after the 1986 election. He told me it was 'nothing personal' he just felt like he needed to, "Follow up on the rumors." I said, "Follow up? Fine. Call me. But file a formal complaint? Really? REALLY?"

I had known for a long time that the Democrat member of my election board had requested to be appointed by his county chairman because he was sure the Republicans cheated. How else could we have always won so many elections? He thought if he got in there, he would see how we did it. Imagine his surprise when he realized that we didn't cheat at all. We worked hard, followed the laws, and did the very best we could for the voters in Marshall County. He could have stopped the ugliness and suspicion—but he didn't. He didn't trust us so he exacerbated the rumors and accusations. When it was all over, I reminded him again, that, if I went down, we all went down. He was as much a part of the process as we two Republicans. After the municipal elections in 1991, on my last day in the clerk's office, he came to me and admitted that he had been wrong—that I was a good clerk and did a really good job with election administration. Too bad It took him seven years to figure it out. It didn't change the fact that I never trusted him again.

I administered five more elections after that 'recount year' and all went relatively smoothly. I never had another recount, and was never again accused of being a 'cheat.' Later, I also ran unopposed for County Auditor—since they couldn't find an opponent for me I guess the Democrats decided I was okay after all.

When my older son, TJ, was in junior high school he became the unofficial 'expert' in all things political. Because of his interest in politics and the election process, I let him come to work with me on election day in 1987. He went in with me at 4:30 AM to get things ready before the poll workers started reporting for work, and stayed with me until we were finished with the canvassing board. He was one tired kid after that day, but he has a tremendous respect for the entire election process, not just the campaign side of it that is extremely partisan. TJ learned from me, and my staff, that it is important to do everything you can to make sure that those who are eligible and have followed all the laws get to cast their vote. In a small community like ours, it is very common to know how people feel politically. Not so much how they vote, of course, but their political leanings. TJ saw first hand that we never treated anyone differently just because we suspected that they might vote differently. My office treated everyone with respect and courtesy, and we were as helpful as we could be. He liked what he saw, and as a result has always treated people exactly like that for his entire life.

Some of the greatest people I worked with came from the state offices that oversaw various aspects of local government. Throughout my sixteen years, I came to know some of them very well and considered them great friends. Since I was active in the various state and regional associations, I often interacted with these folks outside of required meetings.

State Election Board (SEB)

During my holdover year, my predecessor, Mary B, very generously included me in all of the meetings she attended as clerk, giving me an opportunity to meet many of the people I would work with when I actually took office. One of the first meetings we attended was put on by The Indiana State Election Board. The municipal elections were being held that year and there is a statutory requirement that the State Election Board have a training meeting every January of an election year for all clerks and election officials in the state. The clerks and their election deputies attended, other election board members only attended sometimes because most of them were part-time election board and often had full-time jobs.

This meeting took place in Indianapolis and of course the state staff all lived in the Indy area. As we progressed through the meeting, it became more and more obvious that the state staff assumed everyone who came from outside the Indianapolis 'doughnut' (the circle of suburbs that surrounded Indy) had hay in their hair, corn in their teeth, and not many brains. The SEB executive director and the staff attorney were both new to their positions. I'm sure they were learning the ropes too, so they conducted the meetings like we were really stupid and it became more and more frustrating for many of the experienced clerks, especially those coming to the end of their second term. We sucked it up, laughed about it at the evening hospitality rooms, then went home and conducted our elections according to the laws with very few problems.

The following year, 1984, when I was finally in office, was a presidential election year—Reagan was running for reelection. This was a much bigger deal than the town elections had been. Everything had been simple for the municipals, but there is nothing simple about a presidential election. Ever. More candidates, more voter registration, more ballots, more canvassing, more workers, more everything. During the previous year, I had learned a lot about conducting elections, but still had a great deal to learn about a countywide election, especially the presidential. So off I went, with my new election deputy, to the state election board meeting in January, in Indianapolis, with the same state staff.

During that holdover year I had many opportunities to meet other newly elected clerks. Naturally, those of us who started together became really good friends and hung out together at the meetings. The evening of our first day at the election school, several of us went out for a drink in the hotel bar. When we got there, we saw, sitting at another table, the executive director and the attorney from the SEB. They saw us, recognized us as being from their group, and invited us to sit with them. We were all a bit hesitant, because we weren't sure from the meeting if we would like them very well, but we were polite politicians, so we joined them. As the evening progressed we really did enjoy getting to know them better.

However, after we had all become friends, they asked us our opinion of the meetings and could they do anything better. Nobody answered, until I decided that it was an honest question and deserved an honest answer. (Also, I am often very direct, especially when fortified with alcohol). I asked both of them if they really thought all of us who lived outside of the Indianapolis area were as dumb as they portrayed us. Well needless to say, they both were a bit stunned, apologized profusely for coming across that way, and promised to revise their training materials and attitudes. And they both did just that.

Since I'm the one who spoke up, my name was the one they remembered. Of course they eventually got to know all of us, but between my honesty and my many activities around the state, they never forgot me. As the years went by, I actually became quite close friends with the Executive Director.

Two years later was the infamous 'recount' year in Marshall County. That was the sheriff's recount within the congressional recount that caused me so many problems and nightmares. Every election official in the state knew about Marshall County's recounts; most of them just so very glad it wasn't their own county! Since this was the second election in a row that Indiana had congressional recounts, the SEB staff thought this would be a good topic to include in the 1987 election school. Even though it was another municipal election, the director thought it was a good thing for everyone to hear about. So she asked me to share my experiences and thoughts with the group. It was an easy assignment since it was so fresh in my mind; I knew a good many people who would be in the audience and I would have an opportunity to meet new clerks who had been elected the year before. My talk went well; there was a nice question and answer period; and then I went home and began preparations for the upcoming city and town elections.

Then out of nowhere, after the primary election in May, I got a telephone call from a gentleman in the state of Washington inviting me to come to their county auditor's state meeting and conduct a seminar on recounts. In Washington, the county auditors are in charge of the elections. They had read about Indiana's recounts, two years in a row, and contacted the state election board for a speaker. Neither the executive director, nor the SEB attorney were available during that time frame, so they recommended me. He said he would be happy to pay all of my expenses if I would come out there. Needless to say I was flattered, but not sure. I have a family and we had a quick vacation to Disney World scheduled for the few days before the Washington group wanted me. Now my family had been very supportive, and often had to give up something because of my schedule: but Disney World? Are you kidding? Not a chance!! I explained the situation to him, and he offered to have me come a day early to accommodate our schedule. So I agreed.

The vacation was in early June, so we picked our boys up from their last day of school, drove to Indianapolis, got on an airplane, and flew to Orlando. After our vacation, we flew back to Indianapolis, where I kissed my family goodbye, got on a plane to Spokane, Washington, and my family drove home to Plymouth without me. I landed in Spokane, where a nice gentleman met me at the airport and then we drove to Pasko, Washington where the meeting was being held. When we arrived at the hotel, he wanted me to go to the bar with him and meet the people who were waiting for us. They were wonderful folks, as all county officials are, but they had forgotten the time change that occurs. When one goes literally from one end of our vast country to the other in one day—started in Orlando, Florida and ended in Pasko, Washington. I did manage to have a drink, then excused myself, checked into my room, and collapsed.

Since I was included in all of the conference events, I went down to breakfast the next morning, met some of my new friends from the previous evening, and began to see what this was all about. They of course had seminars and meetings all day that had nothing to do with my job as clerk, until that afternoon when the group met to talk about recounts. I gave my spiel as to what had happened in my elections, shared the stories and lessons learned, then threw it open for questions and comments. The one single thread that I noticed was the same all the way across the country—the assumption that recounts and problems are caused by poorly trained election workers at the polls.

Well, that opinion made steam come out of my ears. I don't know of one single, solitary state in this country that has full-time poll workers. It is impossible. We have only a few elections a year and no county can afford to keep poll workers paid full time, we just don't need them enough. So, as a result, the 'volunteer' poll workers come in once or twice a year to conduct the elections on the precinct level and they are not experts. Granted, some work regularly, but sometimes they were the hardest to train because the rules and laws changed from election to election and they didn't want to acknowledge that. I sometimes thought that if I heard again the term 'we never did it like that before' I would jump up and scatter. Generally, all of the workers meant well, but it is really difficult to thoroughly train volunteer workers (they were paid, but not much) for something so important. So everyone does the best they can.

When I explained that to my audience, including a couple from the press, they backed off their criticism a bit and acknowledged that difficulty. Elections are conducted by people, and people are not perfect. Then you throw in some who are extremely political and you add fuel to the possible fire. I sent them instructions in their "thank you for your willingness to serve" letter, docked their pay if they didn't attend a training session, and graciously spent many hours on the telephone, sometimes from home or in my office, talking to workers and answering their questions. And I always tried to remind them, "You may see something at the polls you do not like, but that doesn't make it illegal. You can bring it before the Election Board for action, but we will not take it to court unless a law was broken. Bad behavior and bad judgment are not against the law." It is important to remember that.

After my seminar, I was basically finished for the conference and had another entire free day. In order to save money on the airline tickets, and not having to ask someone to leave the conference early, they asked me to stay the extra day. So I did. I spent it at the pool with some of my new friends, attended the banquet that evening, and just generally enjoyed myself. The next day I was back on an airplane, headed east to my ordinary life of wife, mom, and county clerk. But I will never forget my three days as a 'celebrity' in Pasko, Washington. What fun.

Throughout my reelection and remainder of my two terms as clerk, I continued to work very well with the two main ladies from the state election board. Not long after I moved over to the auditor's office, the SEB executive director took a job with one of the county vendors and we had a wonderful time whenever we saw each other at conferences around the state. If I saw her today we could sit right down, have a beer and talk for hours. She was a neat gal and a wonderful friend during those years.

In Indiana, during an election year, the Clerk of the Court has two full time jobs. The judicial responsibilities do not go away as we work on the elections, But, I was lucky to have great people on both the election staff and judicial staff. There was some talk, over the years, of removing the election responsibilities from the clerk and allowing each county to appoint an election director (like most other states). It would be a full-time job and that would be their only responsibility—administering elections and voter registration. I thought at one time I might like that, but I did love the judicial side of the job too, so it would have been a real toss up for me. However, I didn't have that choice and, as my second term wound down, I began to look forward to starting my new job as Marshall County Auditor.

Chapter 9
Here Comes the Judge(s), the Attorneys, the Plaintiffs, the Respondents, the Defendants, the Prosecutor.....

Ahhh yes, the judicial. Where to start. Clerk of the Courts is just that, the clerk of the court. We had three courts in Marshall County: Circuit Court; Superior Court; and County Court. Eventually, County Court was changed to Superior Court No. 2 so that they could handle all kinds of cases, but it started out primarily as traffic court and small claims court.

County Court/Superior Court No. 2

Like so many courthouses around the state, we were pushed for space, so County Court and the administrative offices for County

Here Comes the Judges... and... and... and...

Court were located in the basement of the courthouse. My office was upstairs and, although I had responsibility for some of the administrative work and all of the financial transactions that went on in that court, I was not directly on site to manage it. It was normal for court staff, Court Administrator, Court Reporter, and Bailiff to be funded through the court budgets since they were employees of the court. However, they did not handle initial filings, court order books, or any money. That was all done in the clerk's office and by the clerk's staff—except in County Court. Our County Court had started with those three staff members, and the clerk had deputized the court administrator to handled the filings and money because it was easier, since she was located downstairs. Unfortunately, as the court cases grew and grew, the court staff was quickly overwhelmed with the 'clerk' duties.

By the time I took office, County Court was handling hundreds of traffic tickets, DUI cases, public intoxication cases, small claim filings, etc. All of those cases involved money, fines and costs, bail postings, filing fees, etc. The court administrator, who had been there from the beginning and was taking care of these cases, was the daughter of my opponent for clerk. I beat her dad, so needless to say she didn't care for me. As a result, communication was not exactly forthcoming from the basement. She did a lot of complaining about being overworked, but then again, everybody did. We were a very busy office.

One day I was downstairs to get a piece of cake (somebody was always celebrating something in the courthouse) and wandered into a back room. I noticed all these boxes full of infraction envelopes (traffic tickets) with checks and money orders attached. WHAT? I looked closer and discovered that some of them went back for months. No, no, no. Money is to be receipted in and deposited by day's end—not months and months later! When I asked what the deal was, the answer was, "I don't have enough time or help." Excuse me? You don't have the time to process payments? Okay, it was time for me to put out this very big bonfire!

I contacted my liaison on the County Council (fiscal body—you will learn about them later) and told him what I had discovered. I told him I wanted my own traffic deputy and I wanted her upstairs in my office. If that was not acceptable, then I wanted a court order from the Judge stating that I was not responsible for all of the monies and filings in County Court. Judge said no, he didn't want the responsibility either. So, a new position was created, we moved all of the desks around yet again, and the deputy clerk position for county court was moved upstairs.

Although that was the long-term solution, and worked quite well, the short-term solution was: Mary Lou took all of those boxes home and sat in the family room, writing receipts and processing all of those tickets and payments. Remember, this was the mid 1980s—no computers in the courts yet, all of it was done by hand. It took me an entire weekend, but when the deposit was made on Monday morning (and I don't remember how many of those little leather bank bags it took.) I was all caught up and we were rolling. Of course, by then my left hand was nearly paralyzed.

In 1986, our county court judge, Rob Bowen, decided to throw his hat in the ring for Indiana Secretary of State. He was a good guy and I really wished him well. His father had been Governor of Indiana, and he would be running against the son of a former US Senator from Indiana, Evan Bayh. It would prove to be an interesting race. However, election law precluded a judge from continuing to serve as judge while running for a different office so he was forced to resign and a new judge was appointed.

Our new judge, Dean Colvin, had been in law enforcement before he went to law school. He was a practicing attorney in St. Joseph

County (South Bend) but was a Marshall County native. He still lived in Marshall County and wanted to come back home to work. He had been in charge of the 'coming on the scene' technology in his law firm, so it was not surprising that he was very interested in automating his court.

I found Judge Colvin very easy to work with, especially after I reminded him that his court operation would run a great deal smoother if there was good cooperation with the clerk's office. Sometimes the judges forgot that we were the central cog that kept it all rolling—at least from my perspective. He agreed to work with me and my staff in trying to find a computer company that would be suitable for our needs. It is very important to remember that in the eighties all the software was custom written. You couldn't really buy 'standard' software for court operations; partly because no one did it that way, and partly because every single court operation ran a bit differently. Even though we all had the same Indiana statutes and trial rules to follow, administration and procedures varied from court to court, county to county, etc. Not easy to standardize anything, let alone software.

But, Judge Colvin did not give up. He found a company in Michigan that wanted to get into the Indiana market. They had a software program that they had written for courts in Michigan and thought they could 'make the minor adjustments' necessary to accommodate Indiana laws. Remember that word, 'minor'. There is nothing 'minor' about computer programming, especially in the crazy judicial world of Indiana. It was decided that we would start with traffic court since that was the largest caseload in all three courts. The judge worked with my traffic deputy and the company, and pretty much hammered out what was needed to be compliant. Then finally it was time to install the software on our computers (we already had two applications in the clerk's office—child support and voter registration) and see if it worked. This was in February and I agreed to go back and enter all of the tickets that had been processed since January 1, so we would have a complete year. My sense of order would not allow me to have six weeks of work dangling out there, so I said I would be the one to do it. Entering all of that data really gave me a sense of how the program worked, what we needed to 'fix', and what we needed to add. Anyone with any experience in working with new software applications (there was plenty of that in those days as computers and the internet came of age), knows it can be very, very frustrating.

Eventually, we moved into the new building, and the software finally did what we needed it to do. It turned out to be a marvelous improvement and we were able to handle hundreds more cases with great ease and efficiency. In fact, many of the state police officers that patrolled our county made sure they stopped people inside our county lines, because they knew the tickets would be properly processed and followed through to payment or driver's license suspension. A nice complement for me and my staff; and as one of my traffic deputies always said, "…It provided lots of job security."

As often is the case, when someone feels that they have been treated unfairly by the judicial system, especially in the case of traffic tickets, they call the traffic desk and want something changed. The only thing we could change was the court date; also known as the 'date your payment is due.' Folks would argue and argue with my deputies about how unfair the ticket was, but there was nothing the deputies could do about it. Inevitably, they would get the 'let me speak to your supervisor' request. So I would pick up the phone and tell the person the very same thing they had already been told dozens of times. Of course, that usually led to the "let me talk to the person you answer to" demand. I had three responses, depending on my mood: 1. "The legislators who passed the law." 2. "My forty-two thousand constituents, which one do you want?" 3. "I only answer to God."

It also really annoyed me when someone would come in to the clerk's office for whatever reason, and fuss and scream at any of my deputies when they didn't get the answer they wanted or get the problem solved. So the gals would come get me, then I would go out and the upset person would be just as nice and sweet and cooperative as they could be. That was so unfair to my staff who had been doing everything they could to help, but were being treated like second class citizens. I always let the person know that I didn't appreciate them treating any of my staff that way. I did every thing I could to have those gals' backs, and when they were wrong, we dealt with it in private—never in front of the world.

Working with judges can occasionally be frustrating, they sometimes forgot that I was an elected official, just like them, and not their employee. However, most of the time we did okay. I especially appreciated the time I went to Judge Colvin and asked him to quit handing out fines and costs to defendants who never pay them. I told him, "I have to record those orders in huge, leather bound books that cost upwards of $300 each (it was the eighties, remember) and take up enormous space. And it's all for nothing, because nobody follows up and makes them pay!" I'll give him credit—he did not realize they were blowing off the court orders, so he added a 'pay by' date every time he ordered fines and costs. If not paid, they were to return to the court and tell him why they were not paid. Didn't take long for word to hit the streets and soon, payments were made on a very regular basis. By the time we automated and got rid of the big books, the payment process had become an accepted standard and was no longer an issue. Bravo Judge Colvin!

Marshall County Circuit Court

When Indiana became a state in 1816, each county did not have a judge, so the few judges available rode the circuit and covered a great deal of territory handling cases. Hence the name, Circuit Court. Eventually each county did have it's own judge and became it's own circuit. Many counties, like mine, had multiple courts, but only one Circuit Court. That is the court that handled most of the more difficult cases: felonies; juvenile matters; divorces; etc. Eventually, Superior Court 1 handled those matters too, but not as much as the Circuit Court.

The Judge in Circuit Court was the late Mike Cook. He swore me in on the first day of my first term and was still there when I left county government sixteen years later. I considered him a great friend and for the most part we worked together very well. We did have some disagreements, mostly about the differences between men and women. Shortly after I started, he asked me if I was one of those 'equal rights women' to which I responded, "...I wasn't sure what he meant. As far as I was concerned, men would never catch up to or be equal to women as far as ability, accomplishment, and general work ethic. So no, they aren't equal and probably never would be." He sort of grinned and said he better get back to work. Touche'.

One time he asked me to come up to the court room to swear in some folks who were testifying for a case. They were from out of town and we were all sitting around waiting for him to arrive. When he got there, he apologized for being late and proudly announced his tardiness had been caused by the birth of his first child, a beautiful baby girl. He boasted that he was sure she would be Miss America someday. I congratulated him and his wife, and then remarked that maybe, better yet, she might be the first female judge in Marshall County... the other folks in the room agreed with me, they were from Chicago. Chicago is a bit more progressive.

Soon after I took office, a huge murder case began in Circuit Court. There was security all over the building (not common in those days) including at the stairway to the court. Only court personnel could have access to the court and court administrative area. The sheriff's deputies were instructed to 'frisk' anyone wanting or needing to go up to that court. Well again, in the days of no security, nobody had badges to wear proclaiming them part of the court system, so the officers didn't always know who we were. Every day when I needed to go upstairs, I waited for them to frisk me... but they never did! I wondered if perhaps I should have been insulted. I have never been frisked. Eventually they began to recognize me as a regular so I quit waiting.

Every once in a while, we would have some high profile cases that brought in more than the local press. It was not unusual to have regional press cover a trial or a story, but on one occasion we had the national press—on a drug case—with a famous local resident.

It is important to note that Plymouth, the county seat in Marshall County, isn't really a large town. At that time the population was probably around twelve thousand, including the surrounding areas that were not incorporated. There was only one high school in Plymouth, so it was not uncommon for students who excelled to be pretty well known. Also, as everyone knows, Indiana is a huge basketball state and in 1982, while I was campaigning for office, Plymouth won the state basketball championship. That was a major accomplishment. This was before the tournament was divided by school size into different classes, and to have a school from a small town like Plymouth winning it all was incredible. (In fact, considering the year this took place, I did a lot of campaigning at the tournament sites).

Well unfortunately, sometime after that, a young man who starred on that championship team, and had gone on to play in the NBA, was arrested for possession of marijuana while he was visiting home. That doesn't seem like a big deal now, but in the mid-eighties it was huge. And because of his ties to the NBA, reporters from all over the country showed up. This was also before the days of cell phones, so the press had no way to call back with their stories except to use the phones in the courthouse. Well sorry, but the phone in the clerk's office was not available to the public so they were forced to go find pay phones. Remember pay phones? In their hurry to file their stories some of them were less than polite. They did not like being told no, they could not use our phone, and called my deputies some interesting names. Then nearly knocked one of them off of the outside steps when she was returning to work from lunch—I was glad we did not have national cases on a regular basis. The regional reporters were mortified by this behavior and asked all of us to remember that it was not them causing the chaos. The young man was eventually found guilty (of a minor charge as I recall) and when he came into my office to pay his fine, my deputies made me wait on him. There were cameras all over the place and I thought I might be on national television, but alas, my footage was edited out, and there went my fifteen minutes of fame!!

However, good things come to those who wait. Just a few years ago, after my son was married, he and his wife were watching one of those shows that goes back and re-investigates open murder cases. It just so happened the case they were investigating took place in Marshall County, and it showed some documents that had been filed in my Circuit Court. It couldn't have been on the screen for more than a few seconds, but TJ immediately recognized *my* signature in the file stamp—and quickly used his phone to take a screen shot of the papers. So it took about thirty years, but at least my name eventually made national television.

One of my favorite things to do, on a time-available basis, was answer inquiries from people all over the country trying to find records of their ancestors. Because we were so busy, I didn't have a lot of time for these requests, but while I was clerk, we were open late on Tuesday evenings, so I would often use that time to do the research. I always stayed on Tuesday to support my staff who was working late, and it generally was a bit quieter in the office at that time.

Most of the old records that I dealt with had to do with marriage records. If you can find it, a marriage license is a real treasure trove of family information. But once in a while I would need to look up a 'dissolution' (divorce) record from the past. It always took me forever because I would start reading through the books and was fascinated by the way some of them were settled. There were more disputes over custody of the dog than over custody of the children. One couple had to split the rows of their garden. And of particular interest to me, if the wife was misbehaving the husband was granted a divorce, pronto, but if he was the bad guy, not so much. I could have sat and spent hours and hours with those old order books. But alas, too much current work to do, however I sure did love the history.

One of the other things we did in the clerk's office was to receive and process the initial filings for the various court cases, including Dissolutions of Marriage. That was an aspect of the marriage business I didn't much care for. But of course we did have some interesting people and divorce cases come in to our front desk.

For example, there was the young man who walked up to the front counter one day about noon. Several of my staff were out to lunch, so I waited on him myself. After I asked how I might help him, he said, "I want a divorce," as if he was just buying a sandwich. He was very nicely dressed and very articulate, so I knew he wasn't stupid. However, it appeared to me that he didn't seem to quite understand how it worked. I explained to him that Indiana didn't require that you have an attorney, but it was probably best to do so if he had children. Yes, he said he had children and asked me for a recommendation of an attorney. Now, that is something I stayed way clear of—I never recommended an attorney because, I knew them too well and I wasn't about to be blamed if things went wrong. Again, no internet, so I suggested he go to the library and look up the members of the local bar association. I often wondered what his wife did to drive him over the wall and make him walk in and ask for a divorce on his lunch hour?

I was also working the front counter one day when an attorney walked in to file a dissolution. And as I began to process the paperwork, I looked at the names—it was a couple who were two of my parents' best friends. Holy smokes! I had grown up with their children, my dad played golf with the husband, my mom played bridge with the wife, and we all went to the same church. They had been married for years and years, their kids were grown, and they were done! Gulp. That was a tough one to handle. Later, after the divorce was final and the settlement entered, if he was late with any payments, she would call me personally to find out why, and ask me to chase it down. I absolutely did not want to get in the middle of all of that, but did my best to help her without getting him too riled up. It was not easy.

Another huge part of the clerk's responsibilities, after a dissolution was final, was handling child support. In those days, all of the payments went through the local clerk's office. The child support records were one of the first areas automated and the software had just been installed when I took office. Mary B's support deputy had worked very hard to get it up and running, and to get all of the records entered, and she agreed to stay and work for me. When

Here Comes the Judges... and... and... and... 123

someone came in to pay support, we would accept their payment, then the system printed their receipt, a check to the recipient, and a copy for our records all as one transaction. Then we signed the check and it went out in that day's mail. Since we could not wait for personal checks to clear, we could not accept personal checks for payment. Mary B had originated the procedure that all payments must be made in cash or by money order. Since the clerk is personally liable for any missing funds, even if it is an error, I didn't hesitate to continue that procedure. However, it did mean a lot of cash went through our office, with a lot of people handling it. All of the staff accepted and processed payments from time to time because the support deputy was not always able to be at her desk. At the end of each day, when it came time to balance the support drawer, and several other cash drawers, no one could leave until we balanced, in case there was an error and we needed to figure out what happened. That was also a great incentive to make sure we all took our time when processing payments—rarely did anybody want to hang around after work!

Of course, anytime a family breaks up because of divorce it is sad, but when kids are involved it can be quite dicey. The ex-wife generally does not think there is enough support ordered; the ex-husband thinks there is too much support ordered; and everyone gets mad at the clerk if it is not paid or received on time!!

The majority of our support payers were men, and the majority of those payers were really good guys who cared about their kids. But not all of them. It was not uncommon for them to come in complaining and carrying on because they had to pay support. One time, I got so frustrated at one fellow for grousing about it all the time, I finally asked him how much he thought it would cost him to be in the home and pay for everything for those kids—house, lights, food, medical, school needs, clothes, activities, etc, etc. I reminded him that I was a mother of school-aged kids; they are expensive and he was getting off pretty good with only having to pay so much per week! And besides, these were his children, if he didn't want to pay for them, he shouldn't have had them! He quit complaining when he came in.

Of course we always had the moms who came in and said they had to have their check right away (we did not hand them out, we only mailed them) because they were desperate for milk and bread, which was code for beer and cigarettes. If we had handed out the checks, there would have been so many gals lined up no one could have gotten into the office; and there probably would have been some knock-down, drag-outs between the exes in the hallway. Best to just use snail mail.

It was not uncommon for an ex-wife to take the ex-husband back to court to have the support amount increased. It was usually based on a change in the husband's income; maybe a promotion, salary increase, whatever. The ex-wife always seemed to know when that happened. One day, we were surprised to read in the paper that a fellow who came in to pay support (always on time, always the correct amount) won the lottery and was an instant millionaire. As one can imagine, the ink was not dry on his lottery check before the ex-wife had him back in court wanting more money. He was a great dad and never minded paying support for his children, so he didn't really mind the increase. One of my deputies got real excited and told him she had never known a millionaire before, and wanted to touch him. He got so tickled that he showed up one day at the office to pay his support and had an ice cream cake for all of us to share. What a sweetheart.

The clerk's office handled every kind of court case filed in Indiana: civil; criminal; probate; juvenile; you name it. We handled all of the money that was paid, including the cash bonds, and any money collected for settlements and judgments. I had an official 'trust' account and that is where we held the money. Money was never disbursed from this trust fund without a court order, no matter what. Often, one of the judges would order attorney fees to be paid out of the cash bond money that a defendant had posted. Every one of the attorneys who practiced law in Marshall County knew I would not give them the fee without the written order, and ninety-nine percent of the time they would wait until the court staff got it processed. However, there was always the exception when an attorney would come in straight from court and give my staff grief because they couldn't have their money right away. One day, I got so frustrated that I told one very impatient lawyer that if he needed me to float him a loan for lunch until we got the order I would be happy to. I didn't want him to go hungry. He gave up.

There were some things that I was 'death' on and would not cut my deputies any slack if they screwed up—issuing arrest warrants was one of those things. An arrest warrant was never, ever, ever to be issued without a signed court order. Sometimes they would know one is coming because of the paperwork and I would let them type it up, but without the signed order, it could not be served. I could count on one hand the number of times that a warrant went out without an order, or was rescinded and still served. In each case that staffer was in trouble. On rare occasions when that happened, and someone came into the courthouse to get it straightened out, I personally walked with them to the appropriate court and stayed with them until the situation was cleared up. Nobody else handled that, not any of my deputies, just me. Sometimes it has to be the boss to taking care of things and these were those times. Fortunately those times were rare.

State Board of Accounts (SBA)

The State Board of Accounts was the agency serving as teachers and trainers, but more than anyone else, they were watchdogs. Not only did they hold and attend meetings for all officeholders all over the state, they also sent field examiners into every county, every office, every year to examine and audit all of the books and procedures. If you have ever had an IRS audit you have the idea of what this is like, only on a scale of about one hundred to one.

My first interaction with an SBA examiner was at the end of my holdover year. I attended the summer clerk's conference with Mary B and of course we went to the hospitality room that evening. Now, the SBA rep who the clerks had worked with for several years was moving to a new position. The clerks, especially the female clerks, were upset to see him leave, they really liked him and they thought he was very good looking. Since I had not established any working relationship with him, I didn't care one way or the other. At one point during the evening, I was getting tired and snagged an empty spot on the couch in the very crowded room. There was a gentleman sitting there alone, so I struck up a conversation. Turns out, he was the replacement for the outgoing examiner and he was feeling kind of bad because the clerks kept telling him how much they were going to miss the other guy. Well I assured him, since I was new at this, that I didn't give a hoot about the other guy, I was very happy to work with him. We sat and chatted on that couch for a long time, drank a few beers together and became fast friends. A few weeks after that meeting, I was attending a funeral for my neighbor across the street and who should come in but my new friend from the state board of accounts. Turns out that the deceased was retired from the SBA (I had forgotten that) and he had trained my new examiner; he had liked and respected his mentor enough to drive up from Indy to attend his funeral.

The next summer, I was in Indianapolis attending the Republican state convention when I went to the hospitality room (I did a lot of hospitality rooms) and my new friend from the SBA walked up behind me at the bar. We sat at a table and chatted again, for a long time. He was a terrific guy and was really helpful to all of us who worked on our single-fee legislation. He often answered questions that he received from the legislators and guided us through the entire process to make sure our changes would fit within SBA rules and guidelines. After a few years he switched over to represent schools and townships, but whenever I called him with a question about anything, he always took my calls and we remained friends until I left office.

I spent eight years working in the judicial system as clerk. I collected and disbursed millions of dollars on behalf of all three courts. I learned the judicial jargon and codes, how to read (and interpret) Indiana laws, trial rules, and court procedures. I worked with attorneys of all stripes—some caring, some kind, some considerate to me and my staff—some not so much. It was not uncommon for an attorney to screw up the paperwork on a case and then 'blame the clerk's office.' Whenever that happened, I would call the attorney and read him the riot act. I will accept responsibility for my own (or my staff's) mistakes, but not some lawyer. I saw a lot of questionable calls from attorneys, and I helped them out of jams more than once. I often commented that I saw the legal community 'from the other side of the counter' and it wasn't always very pretty. But I also had some personal friends who were attorneys in Marshall County and I loved them dearly. I knew I could trust them if I had a legal question or problem that I needed help with. All in all, most of the attorneys were fun, funny, honest, and good to work with.

I was overjoyed when the Marshall County Bar Association finally had a female member—remember, this was in the eighties and female attorneys were not common. By the time I left county government, we actually had three female lawyers, and by then it was the turn of the century—the current century. I'm sure there are more women practicing law in Marshall County by now, and that is a good thing. They still have not elected a female judge; progress is very slow sometimes.

A few years ago I was visiting in Plymouth and a young lady stopped by who had served as one of the court administrators while I was clerk. Several years later she was elected Clerk and told me that I had been her mentor on the proper way to run the office; I was quite touched by that. I know there have been many, many changes over the years—law changes, personnel changes, procedural changes, software changes—and I would probably struggle if I tried to go back and serve again as Clerk. But one thing remains the same, I would do my very best to serve the people in Marshall County, to be loyal to my staff, and be a good a custodian of the judicial records and public funds; just like I tried to do back then.

Chapter 10
Meeting People From All Over the State

It has always been my contention that, if you really want to learn how to do a job, talk with the people who also do that job. Since Indiana doesn't operate local government like most other states—with a professional town, city, or county manager in each locale—professional organizations and associations are vital. These groups provide opportunities for elected officials and their deputies to meet others in the state who do the same job. It was like a 'support group' on steroids. Some of the associations were by districts, some were statewide. By the time we attended both state and district meetings, especially for more then one association, some of us became really, really good friends.

Northern District Clerks' Association

The first organizational meeting that I attended during my holdover year with Mary B, was the Northern District Clerks' Association. The group is made up of all clerks from all of the counties in Indiana located north of Highway 40, which runs east and west through Indianapolis. This was my first introduction to other clerks, and they were amazed that I was attending with my predecessor of the other party. That amazement and incredulity lasted throughout our eight years of working together.

As it turned out, there were several new clerks elected in 1982, and as rookies, we tended to gravitate toward each other. Most of us were in the same party and we all were about the same age. As we became acquainted and began to know each other, a bond was formed with some of them that lasted for more than sixteen years. Since the clerk's office had term limits, many of us continued on in other offices, which allowed us to continue on as friends and colleagues.

Because I am a friendly sort, and somewhat noisy, I soon made many friends in that group. Those who knew and respected Mary B were willing to give me a chance even though I was a different party. In this group I eventually served as Treasurer, and then as President, which gave me the opportunity to meet and work with all of the clerks and many of their deputies, from all across the northern part of the state. When I finished my term as President they gifted me with a beautiful cut glass punch bowl, which I still have and use today.

I'm pleased to say that one of the best meetings our group held was in Marshall County. I agreed to host it and invited everyone to come early, visit our new offices, and check out the new judicial software we were working on. I was so proud of my new space and the progress we were making with technology. We had lots of clerks and their deputies come to the office to check it out. My staff was very gracious to everyone, showing them how everything worked. It was just a great day. As was common, I invited the commissioners and other county officials to join us for lunch, and gave them the opportunity to meet my fellow clerks.

Indiana Association of Clerks of the Court

Needless to say this organization encompassed the clerks in all ninety-two counties. Although I knew the northern clerks better, it meant an opportunity to meet those in the southern part of the state. The clerks' association conference was only held once a year, but it was in addition to the State Election Board training sessions, so we all met in January for elections, and again in early summer for the Clerk's conference.

The State Board of Accounts was required by law to 'call a meeting' of all elected officials, so they did that in conjunction with each separate association. This enabled them to focus on issues pertaining to that particular group. Also, with the association hosting the meeting, other speakers were invited from other areas of clerks' responsibility, such as; elections, judicial, law enforcement, etc. Also, there was always someone in attendance from the Association of Indiana Counties to keep the clerk's updated on AIC activities and lobbying efforts.

This conference was always held in the spring, after the Indiana General Assembly had adjourned. That gave the State Board of Accounts, and others, the opportunity to go over any new legislation that pertained to us. And there was always plenty of that, especially in regards to the judicial and elections.

I never held office in the state clerks' association, but I was very active in their lobbying efforts. In fact, at one meeting, after being told about a whole lot of new fees we were going to have to collect and record for the courts, several of us started talking about the difficulty in keeping track of all those separate fees. The ledger books were already huge (remember, no computers) and balancing them was a nightmare. We wondered if there was a chance the legislators might consider consolidating some of those fees to make it all more manageable.

After the meeting, when we had all returned home, some of us starting working on the possibility of getting some legislation passed. We started meeting in a small group, in each other's courthouses to talk about what we might want. In the meantime, the Executive Director of the Association of Indiana Counties put out some feelers to see if he could find any legislators to carry the bills. We found one of each party in both the House and the Senate. All were attorneys and were well aware of how the clerk's offices operated. But we had to write the bill.

There was a core group of about six of us who worked on the bill consistently. We would put something together, then show it to the legislators, and they would come up with questions or concerns for us to address. We met on our own, we found time at various association meetings, or whenever we could get together and 'hash it over.' Eventually, after many, many meetings, changes, and rewrites, the bill was ready to be submitted for passage and was assigned to the judicial committees of both houses. We made sure we always had someone from our group of authors present when the committees met. We wanted to make sure the questions were answered and information was correct.

After it was put out there for the world to see and read, we ran up against some resistance from the Sheriff's Association. In the past, all 'service fees', in other words, the fees paid for serving papers to someone, had been put in a special fund. That fund was used as life insurance in the case of a police officer being killed in the line of duty. Compromises were made and the sheriffs were finally satisfied. The various legislators who carried the bill did some lobbying; and we were there every time it looked like it would come up for a vote, which it finally did, and it passed. How about that. An idea put together in a clerk's meeting hospitality room became a law. It wasn't easy, but we stayed the course and never gave up. It was a proud day when we all met at the statehouse for the ceremonial signing of the bill by the Governor. We had our picture taken with him while he was signing the bill. Great moment for clerks.

After it was first passed, we watched very closely and as new fees were introduced, we worked with the legislators to build them into the new structure. Of course, as time went by, and we all left office, there was no one in the clerk's offices who knew what collections and bookkeeping had been like before the 'single fee' legislation. So they were not as aware and didn't pay close attention. I noticed when I was Auditor and the money came over from the clerk's office, the fee list just grew and grew. Oh well, we accomplished a great feat, and it did last for a few years. But it is too easy to finance government through extra fees, and the legislators always jump on that so they can campaign that "only the users of the court pay those fees." However, most of the public is completely unaware that they may, and probably will, be users of the court. Not necessarily as hardened criminals, but if they ever get a traffic ticket, want a copy of a court record, get a marriage license, etc. They all come with fees.

After the 1996 election, when I dealt with the double recount, as well as being accused of cheating on the election, I was having a lot of misgivings about continuing as clerk. I had just been re-elected, but I was wondering if this job was really for me. However, when I went to the Association of Indiana Counties' annual conference in December, and attended the clerks' affiliate meeting, I was awarded 'Clerk of the Year' by my peers. This is an award that is compiled from the votes everyone is asked to submit for who they think best represented the clerks around the state that year. I was really, really moved by that award, and thus encouraged to hang in there and not let the negative side of the election drive me away. I will be forever grateful for their vote of confidence that year, and how it helped propel me to continue as clerk, and eventually as auditor.

Needless to say, with all of the meetings, writing legislation, and lobbying, it was very hard to say goodbye to my clerk friends as we ended our terms in office. Fortunately, one of the clerks did not want to say goodbye, so during the fall following everyone's last year in office, she arranged a weekend get together at a camp facility in her county. It was a lodge used in the summer's for juveniles in detention. She set it up with her county officials and we all arrived on a Friday night and left on Sunday afternoon. Everyone took turns, with a partner, carrying in a meal, and we just 'hung out' together and talked, and laughed and laughed and laughed. By this time, many of us had moved onto other offices, a couple of us to the same position which allowed us to still get together frequently. Those were very special weekends with very special friends and we continued to do it for several years. I made new friends as I moved on and met new people, but there was always a soft spot in my heart for those clerks and our weekends at the lodge.

In December of 1991, as I was concluding my second term as Clerk, I wrote this poem and sent it to the clerks around the state who I had been closest to. I think it pretty well sums up the affection that I felt for all of those colleagues I got to know so well over the eight years that I served as Clerk of the Marshall Circuit Court.

MARY LOU LEAVELL
CLERK MARSHALL CIRCUIT COURT
211 W. MADISON ST.
PLYMOUTH, INDIANA 46563

TO THE LADIES OF THE EIGHTIES

I'M SITTING HERE THINKING AS MY TERM COMES TO AN END
HOW MANY FELLOW HOOSIERS I CAN NOW CALL MY FRIEND.
WHEN I RAN FOR THIS OFFICE HEEDING MY PARTY'S CALL,
I HAD NO IDEA WHAT IT WOULD BE LIKE AT ALL.

WE LOBBIED & LAUGHED, AND SCREAMED IN FRUSTRATION
PLANNING & PREPARING WITH LATE NIGHT CONSTERNATION.
REMOVE LIABILITY, ADD CENTRAL COUNTING, SINGLE FEE
SO MANY HOURS AND TRIPS TO INDY, AND WE DID IT FOR FREE!

AS WE TRAVELED INDIANA TO ATTEND ALL THE MEETINGS
WE ALWAYS KNEW THERE WOULD BE LOTS OF WARM FRIENDLY GREETINGS.
WHAT WOULD WE HAVE DONE WITHOUT NEMETH & PRIDE
THEY WORKED SO CLOSE WITH US, ALWAYS ON OUR SIDE.

ELECTIONS - OH MY - A WHOLE OTHER CHAPTER
WE COULD NEVER SURVIVE THEM WITHOUT LOTS OF LAUGHTER.
WE REGISTERED VOTERS, DID BALLOTS, HELPED ABSENTEES
THEN GOT THE PHONE CALL "SO I MOVED - LET ME VOTE... PLEASE".

WE PUT OUR RECORDS IN ORDER AND PROPERLY PURGED
JUST TO HAVE DEPUTY REGISTRARS DESCEND WITH THEIR SURGE
WE WORKED HARD ON ELECTION DAY, STARTING AT DAWN
ONLY TO BE QUESTIONED ON WEDNESDAY "HOW COME THE OTHER GUY WON"?

WE TRAINED PRECINCT WORKERS AND THEN WE WOULD PRAY
THE FORMS BE DONE CORRECTLY AND TURNED IN THAT WAY.
THERE WAS ONE MORE PRAYER AS THE TENSION WOULD MOUNT
PLEASE LET 7 DAYS PASS WITHOUT A RECOUNT!!

WE TAKE IN FINES FOR THE STATE, SMALL CLAIMS FOR THE SCHOOLS
SPEND TIME TEACHING JUDGES & LAWYERS THE RULES.
WE MICROFILM RECORDS, KEEP JUDGMENTS, THE RJO
AND OF COURSE "IS MY SUPPORT THERE? - I'M SORRY MA'AM, NO"

I CAN ONLY REMEMBER WITH A GOOD HEARTY LAUGH
ALL THE HOURS WE SPENT TRYING TO SOLVE PROBLEMS WITH STAFF
THE DUTIES WE HANDLE ARE TOO MANY EACH DAY
TO REALLY TRY TO LIST IN ANY GOOD WAY.

I'VE NEVER WORKED HARDER AT A JOB IN MY LIFE
WITH SO MANY UPS & DOWNS, SO MUCH LAUGHTER & STRIFE
I'M RELIEVED TO BE FINISHED BUT THERE WILL ALWAYS LURK
WAY DOWN IN MY MEMORY MY YEARS AS...THE CLERK!!

IT'S BEEN EIGHT YEARS, OH HOW THE TIME FLIES
WE SAID SO LONG AT AIC WITH TEARS IN OUR EYES
WE SHARED A GREAT ADVENTURE, THAT HAS MEANT SO MUCH
SO PLEASE FRIENDS, LET'S MAKE THE EFFORT TO NOT LOSE TOUCH!!

My Christmas greeting to my clerk friends; December 1991

Chapter 10
New Digs Are Necessary

One of the things I liked about the clerk's office was working in the stately old courthouse. One of the most difficult things about the clerk's office was working in the stately old courthouse.

The Marshall County courthouse was built in the mid-nineteenth century for one court and the original county offices created by the constitution; Clerk, Auditor, Treasurer, Assessor, and Recorder. It also housed the circuit court room and court staff. Not much had changed when Tom and I moved to Marshall County in April of 1971. One thing we all know for certain, government on all levels grows and grows so it wasn't surprising when Marshall County ran out of room in the courthouse. In 1973 a second court was established, Superior Court No 1, so the first real renovations in the courthouse were made to accommodate that court. A new jail was built in the early seventies and some of the county offices were moved from the courthouse to the basement of the jail. Well, it wasn't long until the jail needed that space back, especially for their emergency response operation, so in the mid seventies a new county office building was built across the street from the courthouse. This freed up some space in the courthouse for the third court room that was established in 1975, and expanded the space needed for the clerk's office into two rooms. As a result, the only offices now in the courthouse were the clerk's office and the three courts.

But again, government keeps growing and growing, so before too long, the courthouse once again was too small. And, to make matters worse, over the years the stately old building was not kept up as it should have been. Exterior work was done, but not much to the interior. One of the biggest problems was the wiring. Remember, when the Marshall County courthouse was built in the early eighteen seventies, there were no computers, certainly no space heaters, and no lights. I suspect that over the years, the building was wired on an 'as needed' basis, which caused quite a bit of inconvenience with future needs.

For example, the circuit courtroom on the second floor was exceptionally cold in the winter. When Judge Cook needed to be on the bench for long periods of time, he used a space heater under the bench to keep his feet warm. Problem was, every time he turned on the heater it tripped the circuit breaker and I lost 'juice' to a whole row of desks. There went the typewriters, adding machines, (remember, this was the eighties, no computers on every desk just yet) and anything else 'plugged' in. So, I would run to the basement and reset the circuit breaker. I asked the judge to just call me when he was going to turn on his heater, so we could turn off our appliances for a moment. He agreed, and always forgot.

There was a maintenance staff, and they were also supposed to do some cleaning, but they didn't really do much of either. It was made up of a couple of retired fellows who generally took naps in the basement of the county building (I know, I caught them there) and a nice man with some developmental issues who was guided by the old guys, so he didn't do much either. One day we were having a lot of trouble with the electrical outlets along one row of desks. We called maintenance (heaven forbid we call an electrician and incur an expense) so the two of them came in to check out the situation. They removed the cap from the floor outlet and began poking around. I suggested that perhaps they might want to turn off the juice to that row of outlets, but they just laughed at me. Wasn't long until one of them stuck their screwdriver clear into the outlet and sparks were flying four feet high. Looked like a fireworks ground display. Those women sitting there moved faster than I had ever seen them move. To this day I don't know how we managed to keep all the papers on the desks from catching on fire, not to mention the guys getting completely fried. Of course, THEN we called the electrician who came in and fixed the problem for a reasonable fee. The black spot on the carpet was there until the day we moved and they remodeled the office for the court staff.

People in the midwest do a great deal of complaining, justifiably, about their weather patterns, The inconsistency, the extreme hot, extreme cold, cloudy days, etc. But one thing you could count on were some gorgeous fall days. And on those days there is nothing better than a room full of fresh air. The girls loved to open the windows in the office and let that air in, but unfortunately with the fresh air came bees, flies, and general critters. There were no screens on the windows. A couple of the gals who had desks near the windows brought in those screen inserts (paid for by themselves personally) so they could open the windows without bugs, but the bugs still seemed to get in. No matter, we loved our beautiful fall days in Indiana and kept the windows open anyway.

We worked around the weather the best we could, froze in the winter and suffocated in the summer. Yes, the courthouse had heat and air conditioning, but it always worked way better in the hall than in the office. If we propped open the front door to let in the heat or air conditioning we wouldn't always hear someone come in. So, I thought I had the best solution. I bought one of those doorbell mats that rings when you step on it. Just a couple of problems with that—it rang when someone came in, which was the point; but it also rang when someone when out—and Judge Cook loved to come in the office and stomp on it over and over to make it ring, and ring, and ring. Real funny. Wasn't long until the doorbell mat disappeared and there was a collective sigh of relief, not to mention quiet.

But the one thing nobody could fix in the office was the cramped conditions. So as caseloads increased, technology came on the scene, and staff size grew, we were forever rearranging furniture and moving things around to make it more efficient. To quote an auditor friend of mine from another county, who also worked in an overcrowded office, my staff was sitting 'tit to tit and butt to butt.' Along one side of the office was a bookcase on top of a counter on top of a row of low filing cabinets that ran the length of the wall. The bookcase was designed to house the great big leather bound books required by law to keep the court records. These books were public record and often had researchers standing at that counter going through them, not to mention my staff when they needed to put entries in them. It was a well-designed space, except as the office grew, the other furniture encroached on the space in front of the counter. If someone was standing at the counter, another person could not get by them. A whole lot of staff time was wasted over the years as people stopped, stepped back, and got out of the way for another person to pass, dozens of times a day.

Fridays were the busiest days in the clerk's office because it was often 'payday' for support payers, we had DUI court and family court, and many attorneys liked to get cases filed before the weekend. One Friday afternoon, I happened to be leaning against the main counter with my back to the front door, facing my staff. The office was just buzzing with people, ringing phones, typewriters clacking, and general activity. An attorney friend of mine walked in the door, came up behind me and said, "This looks like the station house on the TV show Hill Street Blues" (a popular police show in the eighties). I laughed, but thought, boy is he right, total controlled chaos. Because of our limited space needs I was always talking to the county commissioners about possible ideas to solve the problem. One busy Friday, the chairman of the commissioners came into the office and just sat down on a chair in the back of the room. He didn't say much and I realized he was there to observe. Not to 'check on us,' he wasn't that kind of guy, but to see what I meant by 'space needs.' He quietly observed for nearly an hour, then came over to me, shook his head and said, "I don't know how you do it." But, nothing changed.

As frustrated as I was about the lack of space, deterioration of the building in the offices also played into the problems. Eventually a small 'soft spot' in the ceiling of my front office began to grow. A little bit of plaster fell onto the counter, then a little bit more, then a little bit more. I brought it to the commissioners' attention, but nothing happened. At one point I threatened to put a stack of multi-colored hard hats on the counter and make anyone who came in put one on for their own protection. Pretty soon it started dripping, so of course we had to have the requisite 'bucket' on the floor to catch the drips. We didn't have a break room in the office, but we did have a coffee pot. To fill the carafe I used to have to go out in the hall to drinking fountain, but one day I suggested to my staff that we could save time if we just stood there and 'caught' the drips into the carafe instead of going on out to the fountain. Apparently one day the drip got big enough, I suppose the wrong person fell over the 'drip bucket' and complained to the commissioners, so they finally had the ceiling repaired. They certainly didn't do it for me, or any of my staff.

New Digs Are Necessary 141

Because of the never-ending search for more space, I spent a great deal of time trying to create more work areas. I had the front counter redesigned and moved the child support deputy into an unused corner, which made it easier for payers to get in and out. I also used the high ceilings in the back room to install a mezzanine for storage. Tom and I had a friend who sold industrial storage solutions and I asked him one time if something like that might work in the courthouse. He came to my office to check it out and do some measuring. He determined what would fit, then he gave me a price quote. I went to the commissioners and asked permission to have this installed in the back room. It would mean moving a great many of the large historical books to the basement of the county building, moving the marriage licenses and judgment books we used for research up on the new mezzanine, and installing a microfiche machine (no Google in those days) for research. I paid for the mezzanine with my IV-D money, (explained in another chapter) it did not come out of the county's general fund budget, and my friend installed it for nothing. We used county jail inmates to move the books (I unlocked the coke machine and let them help themselves since it was hot, hard work), and I was able to add three more work spaces in the back room, including room for my desk. (When we moved to the new facility I gave the mezzanine to the highway department for storage).

There was a small, two-room empty office in the county building that I asked to use for the election office. The commissioners agreed, so I moved the entire voter registration and election processes into that space. Offices in two separate buildings was a real pain and of course meant that I was invariably in the wrong office from where I was needed.

By the time I completed the changes, I had created a total of four new work spaces in the court house. Pretty good, I always thought.

The courthouse deterioration and space needs got so bad that the circuit court judge met with the county commissioners, who were in charge of the buildings, and told them if they did not come up with a solution on their own, he was going to order them to build a new building. Remember, you blow off a court order, you get arrested for contempt. They were not inclined to go to jail.

The commissioners hired the architectural firm that designed the county building and began to make plans for an addition to the courthouse, I never cared for the solution they came up with, I thought it looked like a boil on the beautiful courthouse building, but I did work to plan my space and make sure it met our needs, including lots of extra computer ports, even though everyone said I was crazy because we would never have that many computers. Ha!

One of the things that concerned me as the construction of the new facility progressed, was what would we do about furniture? The desks in the clerk's office were old, old Steelcase desks, the kinds with the typewriter platform (before electric typewriters) that slid out of sight when you didn't need to type. They were beat up, too small, and extremely outdated. It seemed such a shame to move to that beautiful new building with those crummy desks. At this point, it is important to note that, when I took office as clerk, I brought my own desk. Mary B didn't have one; she had given it to a deputy when they hired an additional person and there was nowhere for the new lady to sit. So Mary worked wherever she could find a spot, a table, counter, etc. Not a good way for an elected official in charge of such a large operation to work. Just before I took office, my husband moved his office into a former law office, which had 'built in' furniture, So, I charmed a couple of those attorneys into bringing my husband's old desk up to the clerk's office for me to use. I was not as tolerant as Mary and I wanted my own desk. It was no surprise to me that the commissioners were oblivious to the furniture needs for the new building, so I knew it would be up to me to figure it out, just like I did when creating more work space.

I checked with several vendors of office products and furniture, and got several price quotes on what I thought I would need. We built in work spaces at the front counter, (no desks needed there) and what would become the traffic desk (no desks needed there either). That left us needing five new desks and new furniture for me. I added an extra desk for potential growth that we used exclusively for marriage license preparation. That way no one had to 'move aside' their work to meet with a couple and type up a marriage license. I had enough money in my IV-D funds, (the same money I used to build the mezzanine) to purchase all of the furniture, and a new coffee pot for the break room. I selected the best quote for nice oak desks and had them delivered when we moved in. The salesman who sold me the furniture came and stayed all day helping to put them together. I added a credenza and two-drawer file for my office and bought a nice executive desk chair. I found a small antique table in the attic at the courthouse, had it refinished, and put that in my office, also. I convinced the commissioners to hire someone to put a new coat of paint on all of the filing cabinets to clean them up and make them match the counters. When they were painted, the cabinets looked brand new and really fit in well. I found some of the old-time, skinny drawer cabinets in the county building that were a perfect fit for the traffic infraction envelopes. Those cabinets were painted and installed with a counter on top, and it became a wonderful work space for the traffic deputies.

I worked very closely with the architectural firm on the design of the clerk's office. I did not want extravagant, but I did want efficient and attractive. I had windows put in the private office so that I could see the traffic desk and the entire outer office, and they could see me. That afforded me the privacy and quiet I needed to work, and allowed me to still know what was going on all the time. I hung my various plaques, awards, and the architects rendering for the building (a gift from my deputies) in the office for decoration. It made a very nice place to work and we did it all at no additional cost to the county.

I thought it might be a good idea to have a 'drive-up' window, like a bank, for support payers. We could allow for night deposits and then they could pay anytime over the weekend. Well, the building wasn't situated in such a way to have a drive-up window, but we were able to have a drop-in window by the sidewalk. We kept envelopes handy for them to put their name and payer number, and it was a very popular feature. The first thing each morning, especially on Mondays, we would get the payments out of the safe and process them. It cut down on traffic at our counter and made life a great deal easier for the guys who were paid on Friday and couldn't get their money orders in time to get to the clerk's office. Everybody was happy; a rare occurrence with the public.

We moved into the new building in early 1988 and moved the election office back over with the main clerk's office. It was airy, roomy, bright, and I finally had a private office of my own, something I had never had in the old courthouse. And best of all, we never had to rearrange the furniture again, everyone had plenty of room!

I'm sure there have been some changes to the clerk's office, it has been many years since I have been there, but I tried my best to design and decorate it in such a way to meet the test of time. I stayed away from 'trendy' colors and materials knowing that county officials are not inclined to redecorate any of the offices just to keep them up to date. I like to think that is part of of my legacy to the Marshall County judicial system, plus Mary B made them put my name on the dedication plaque (they left it off the first time and she made them redo it) because I had worked so hard to make the office a great place to come to work.

I know each subsequent clerk made changes, especially to the private office. My successor took out the pretty antique table and added a couch. He thought if someone didn't feel well or was tired it would nice for them to have a place to lie down. (Sorry, when my staff didn't feel well I made them take a sick day, sleeping or resting on county time was not acceptable). Also, he installed a bank of security monitors so he could watch the ladies who worked in the basement—apparently he didn't trust them. I suppose those things are still there, and other things have probably been changed, but overall, the clerk's office was a nice facility when I we moved in and I hope it still is.

The top two floors of the new Courts building were court facilities, one court room for Superior Court No. 2, formerly housed in the basement of the court house, and an extra court room for growth or special judge cases. After we vacated the space in the courthouse, work began on remodeling that space for the Superior Court No. 1 offices and some changes to the courtroom. Superior Court 1 also moved across the street to their temporary digs (formerly the commissioners meeting room) until their remodeled facility in the old courthouse was completed. Work also began on the Circuit Court facilities in the old courthouse and they used the newly-created extra office in the new courts building while their facilities in the old courthouse were being renovated. It was another year before everyone moved back to where they should be, but it was well worth the effort. Eventually, Superior Court No. 1 moved into the court room on the third floor of the new courts building and the vacant court room in the old courthouse was used for overflow and special judge cases. The former court staff offices were used by Court Services. It is my understanding that the county is trying to obtain a fourth court which requires approval of the Indiana General Assembly. If they are able to expand to a fourth court, they already have the facilities they will need because of their careful planning for the future.

It had always been 'a given' that I would run for Auditor. It was really the only way I could stay in office and not have to resign my last year as Clerk. I loved the clerk's office, the judicial, the elections, all the weddings, etc; however I was a bit apprehensive about the Auditor's job. From my side of the street, it seemed like it was extremely difficult. Mary B continually assured me that I would have no trouble being Auditor. (She really shouldn't have encouraged me that much since she was of the opposite party, but as I mentioned before, we just didn't work that way). I had a pretty good reputation as Clerk so when I filed as a candidate for Auditor I was fortunate to be able to run unopposed. That was nice since I was still conducting the elections and wouldn't have to add the extra work of campaigning to my already very long days. By this time, TJ was in high school and very active. There was no time for a campaign when every weekend is taken up watching varsity football or judging speech meets. Steve was still in junior high, so he was not yet quite so busy.

County Auditor is the other holdover office, so after the election, Mary was adamant that I go with her to all of the meetings and meet her auditor friends, just like we had done when I was elected clerk. Some of them I already knew from my own state activities, but it was great to meet the others, attend the meetings, and begin to get a handle on the job. And yes, I offered the same courtesy to my successor in the clerks office, a Democrat. I took him to every meeting I attended and introduced him around. He wasn't quite as comfortable accepting the political differences as I was, but he did go with me and make the effort to meet everyone.

New Digs Are Necessary 147

In December of 1992, after I completed the 1991 municipal elections, I began to clean out my office and look forward to my new job in the county building. It was a little bittersweet having to leave the office that I helped design, decorate, and fight for. I was the first clerk to work in that space, so I will always consider the clerk's facilities in the Marshall County Courts building 'my office.'

Being sworn in by Circuit Court Judge Michael Cook. County Court Judge Rob Bowen is in the background.

The infamous airplane wedding. Me exiting the plane, with the pilot/groom standing behind the wing and my boys in front. Maid of honor is on the left.

The final marriage I performed on my last day as Clerk.

With my election board. Ollie Greer (R) on my right and George Davis (D) on my left.

Training election precinct workers at my first general election in 1984. (The Pilot News *clipping*)

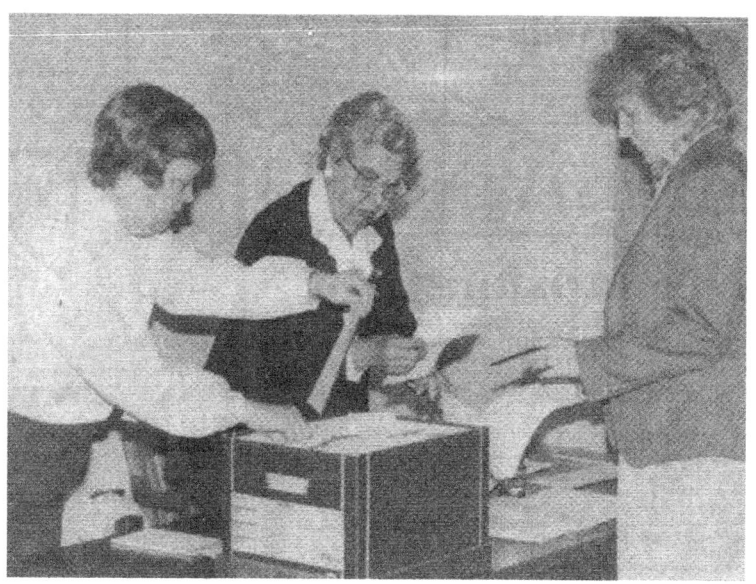

Packing the voting materials for the traveling absentee voting team in the 1984 General election. (The Pilot News *clipping*)

The election board during the 1986 recount. Hayden Patz (R) on my left and Art Hiester (D) on my right. (The Pilot News *clipping*)

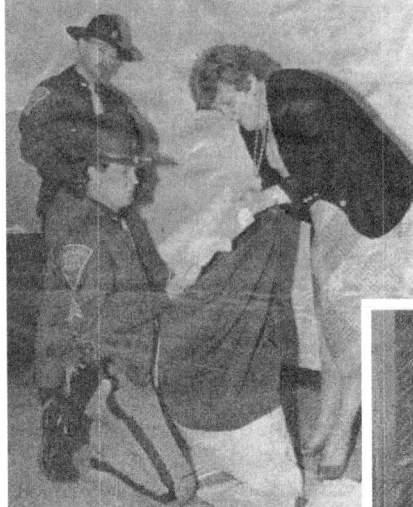

My new best friends—two state police officers helping me pack up the ballots to be taken to the ISP headquarters in Bremen before the 1986 Investigation. (The Pilot News *clipping*)

Locking up the election office. I couldn't get in there for three months, all the plants died. (The Pilot News *clipping*)

Investigation produces no wrongdoing in '86 election

Headline announcing that the 1986 cheating accusations were false—just like I told everyone!! Nice for it to be right on the front page of the paper, in big, bold letters. (The Pilot News *clipping*)

Tom and I on Friday night 'helping' our friend install the mezzanine in the court house to make more room for my deputies.

The very sweet note I received from the Thurston County Auditor in Washington after I spoke at their state meeting.

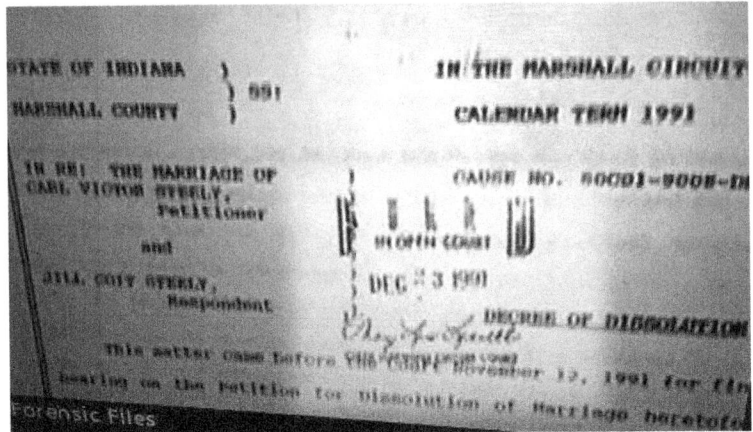

My thirty seconds of national fame. My file stamp on documents shown on the TV show Forensic Files. *TJ and his wife, Jerilyn were watching and it was incredible that he recognized it so quickly—it was only on for a few seconds.*

The official signing of HEA 1183 with Gov. Robert Orr. The bill's sponsors are in the back on the ends. I am in the first row on the left, the others are my fellow clerks on the legislative committee and our AIC representative in back row, second from left.

Touring the new courts building construction with Commissioner Clark Dare. I was showing him where my office would be.

The back wall of my office in the new Courts Building. Check out the old computer and giant dot-matrix printer!! So modern for the times.

The outer office of the new clerk's office in the Courts Building. That is the wall of books we 'recreated' from the old court house.

Me, back row right, with all of my deputy clerks on my last day in office, December 31, 1991.

Part 3 - Marshall County Auditor

"Find the smartest people you can and surround yourself with them."

—Marissa Meyer

Chapter 12
Goodbye Courts Building, Hello County Building

My first official act as County Auditor was to rearrange the furniture.

When the county building was built in the mid-seventies, for some reason there were no private offices for some of the office holders, directors, or whatever—in other words, the boss. Neither the County Auditor or the County Treasurer had a private office. Well, that was just unacceptable to me.

There was a small conference room in the auditor's office that was very rarely used. All the meetings took place in the adjoining commissioner's room. So, I decided to turn that small conference room into my private office. My predecessor, Mary B, retired when her term as Auditor ended, so she left shortly after Christmas. She had given me the key to the office so that I could go ahead and begin to move in. My husband, Tom, and son TJ, went with me to the office on New Year's Day to set up the office the way I wanted it, while nobody else was around.

Since there was no private office, there was no office furniture. However, there were some unused counters in a third floor space. So we went upstairs and snagged those counters and placed them all the way around the walls in a 'U' shape, and used the small conference table as a desk for me. Since there weren't any drawers in the table, we moved in two 2-drawer filing cabinets and put them next to the table. We moved some tall filing cabinets that Mary B had used behind her desk (that housed her files), into the office and brought in a small bookcase from home for me to display some of my 'pretties' from the clerk's office. We used the conference room chairs for guest chairs and my desk chair, and Tom hung my pictures from the clerk's office in my new office and 'voila'—I had my own private space (again, with no additional cost to the county). The counters we brought in were lower than desktops so I put my computer there (desktop computers were very large in those days), with the printer next to it. That left the desk with lots of room for work space. It really was nice digs.

Of course, the next day when the world went back to work after the New Year holiday, there were some very stunned people. The deputies who came with me from the clerk's office were not surprised. They were very used to my need for organization. However, the gals who were already there, and some of the other officeholders in the building were quite surprised. I don't think they were ready for me to waltz in and take charge. Don't know why—just because I had not previously worked in their building didn't mean I had changed my stripes.

Probably one of my most important assets is my organizational skills. When I was clerk I had a series of 'cubbies' built and labeled for each election precinct. Then, as I was working the election I could 'sort' as I went, putting things in the appropriate precinct; i.e., absentee ballot applications, lists of precinct workers, etc. Anything that was germane to that individual precinct.

Well, it was the same for the commissioners and council members. Instead of having larger cubbies built, I set up a series of plastic stacking trays and sorted as I went. Then, when it came time to disburse those materials I never had to 'search' or worry that I had enough copies, etc. It really worked very well.

Since the Auditor's office was the 'hub' of county government, I did the same thing with stacking trays for all of the offices in the county, and put them by the front door. Anything that needed to be distributed to a county office, or all of them, from notices to paychecks went into those trays. As county personnel came in and out of the office, they eventually learned to check those trays. It was a great system and much appreciated by all of my colleagues around the county.

When I started my tenure as auditor I did the same thing I had done when I started as clerk. I accepted that I had a lot to learn and jumped right in. I spent many hours, (mostly on my own time) studying statutes, procedural manuals from the state, and reading through old minutes to get a sense of what issues were ongoing and what issues were settled. Eventually, my colleagues throughout the county, other elected officials, department heads, and employees, began to realize that I was trying very hard to learn and if I didn't know an answer, I would look it up, not make it up. Hence, they were willing to trust me.

The auditor's offices around the state became the 'hub' of the county by default because Indiana does not have county managers.

My range of duties included many things that affected all of the other offices. These various duties included:

- Secretary to the County Commissioners
- County fiscal officer and secretary to the County Council
- Payroll and all HR duties for all county employees
- Paying all of the claims (bills) for the entire county
- Receiving all non-tax revenue from the various offices that collected money
- Distributing all taxes and miscellaneous revenue to other political sub-divisions twice a year
- Keeping track of property records for all county residents and businesses
- Secretary to the Job Classification Committee
- Secretary to the Board of Review
- Served on the Technology Committee
- Served on the Old Records Committee

Obviously, the auditor's job is extremely complicated and varied, which is why it was so interesting and I loved it so much. I had loved my work as clerk—interacting with the public, other officeholders, the judicial, etc—but as auditor, I was totally immersed in the day-to-day work of county government; elected colleagues, department heads, county employees, school administrators, librarians, city clerks, township trustees, realtors, real estate title researchers, bankers, you name it. When they needed something, they all started with the Auditor's office. And then of course; there was the public, although there isn't as much public traffic in and out of the auditor's office as there was in the clerk's office, it was still a very busy place.

When the county building was new, the people in charge at that time made the decisions about what each office looked like. As I mentioned, when the new clerk's office was being built, I decorated the office in a way that would not become 'outdated.' I wish they would have done that in the county building also. Having run in and out of the that building and noticing the colors, I knew the powers that be (commissioners) would not spend money on redecorating. There was lots of rust, orange, lime green, lemon yellow, brown, and beige. Every morning when I went to work, I felt like I was fifteen years younger because my environment screamed nineteen seventies. I eventually got used to the colors, but would bet they are the same today, more than twenty years later. Oh well, everything comes back in style sooner or later.

Chapter 13
Mary Lou and Her Boys

A huge part of the Auditor's job is secretary to the Board of County Commissioners, the county executive branch. Again, since Indiana does not have a 'county manager' form of government, that responsibility often fell to the auditor, mainly because of the close association with the board of commissioners.

There are three elected county commissioners, each from their own district, however they are elected by the entire county. They serve four-year terms and do not have term limits. It is not uncommon to have someone serve as a commissioner for many years. However, because they are part time, they just don't have the in-depth knowledge of the full-time office holders, and they rely very heavily on the Auditor. Now, that can be a double-edged sword.

On one hand, I always knew what was going on in the county; most of the major decisions, except for budgeting, went through the commissioners and I served as their secretary. Unfortunately, they often forgot that, in this case, secretary was not synonymous with employee. I was an elected official just like them. They were my colleagues, not my boss. As new commissioners were elected, it was not uncommon for me to have to remind them of this fact, usually after they had 'instructed' me to do something that I could not do. I often heard the statement, "You'll do it if I tell you to" and my response was, "Oh no I won't, I took the same oath you did." Then I would prove my case with little things such as laws, ordinances, procedures, and other legalities. Inevitably, whichever one was 'bossing' me at the time would back off and accept my position.

For the most part I got along and worked well with the commissioners. Most of them really appreciated my organizational skills and knew they could get whatever information from me they needed, and usually rather quickly. Over the years, I learned to take very detailed minutes—even though I also tape-recorded each meeting—and I tried really hard to have the minutes typed up and distributed to them a week before their next meeting.

A large part of commissioner meetings were the people who came before the board with specific requests. Many of the them were department heads who came to give their monthly report, or to make a special request. (Any non-elected department head was appointed by the commissioners.) Since I set the agenda for the meetings, all of those people would have to go through me first, so I always knew what was happening and what they wanted. Many elected officials came before the board with specific requests that fell under the purview of the board, or sometimes just to get advice on how they might want to handle a problem. The commissioners met twice a month, so that was a huge part of my job. After each meeting, I did all of the follow-up that was needed, in addition to the minutes, and sometimes there was a lot of work after an all-day meeting. The second meeting of the month was only a half day, as they met with the Surveyor in the morning to work on drainage issues.

Since the auditor and the commissioners worked so closely together, we attended many meetings outside of the courthouse. Our county was a member of the Indiana County Commissioners Association and the commissioners almost always attended all of those district and annual meetings. They also attended the Association of Indiana Counties (AIC) Northwest District meetings, and the AIC annual meeting. These meetings included social hours and dinners, as well as presentations regarding new legislation, statewide projects, etc. The annual meetings were held for two or three days, and included instructional classes as well. These meetings were also attended by many vendors, because commissioners made purchasing decisions, construction decisions, personnel decisions, just about everything except budgeting, so the vendors were always present to pitch their wares. Most of those folks were really very nice and we all got to know them pretty well, sometimes even on a personal basis.

Indiana is not a huge state, and with only ninety-two counties it was easy to keep track of the elected officials, especially since the commissioners often served for many years. Until my last years as auditor we only had male commissioners in Marshall County. Around the state, we were often referred to as "Mary Lou and her boys."

Even though the commissioners were my colleagues, I didn't have the authority to make decisions. Of course, I was always happy to 'weigh in' with my opinions; sometimes that was appreciated, sometimes not; but almost never with the county attorney. During board meetings, we usually took a break and went up to the third floor employees lounge for coffee. I learned that this was the time to express my opinion. I did always try to be respectful during the meetings and not say anything in public. Those meetings were covered by the press and I didn't really have any interest in causing trouble or embarrassing anyone.

Also, the first meeting of the month was an all-day affair, so we broke at noon and went out to the county home for lunch. The county home was under the administration of the commissioners and they were required by law to do a monthly inspection. This lunch gave them an opportunity to meet with the administrator, consider any concerns, and do a 'walk around' of the building as required in the statutes. I enjoyed these lunches; the food was good, I liked visiting with the residents, and it was private enough to discuss things, but not in violation of open door laws because they never made any decisions at those lunches.

In the early days, the county home was referred to as the county farm. Our county home, called Shady Rest, was a beautiful old, stately mansion built in the nineteenth century.

Of course it had been updated, especially the interior, and the grounds and the exterior were meticulously maintained. Originally it had been a farming operation and housed indigent or developmentally disabled folks. The farm sustained itself and provided a certain income to the county. Eventually the county stopped farming and rented the land to local farmers (determined by the bid process). County farms were common in the mid-west in those days, but by the late twentieth century, there were very few still operating. In 2002, a couple of years after I left the auditor's office, the commissioners transferred the farm deed to the Bowen Center, a facility for the treatment of addictions and mental illness, both out patients and residential patients. The Bowen Center operated the facility for fifteen years, then informed the commissioners that Shady Rest no longer met the federal standards for medicaid and medicare. As a result, they would need to turn the facility back over to the county. In 2018, the commissioners again transferred the deed, (with the same basic arrangements they had with the Bowen Center) to David's Courage, a faith-based transitional home for drug and alcohol addiction treatment.

As the executive body of the county, the commissioners took care of the business of the county. It was their responsibility to approve all contracts, and even though some other officeholders needed contracts within their particular purview, the contract still had to be approved by the commissioners. So it would be up to the county attorney to review the contracts, and me to keep track of them.

The commissioners were responsible for all things employee-related, except salaries. They set the various employee policies like number of work days and hours, vacation time, and sick days, etc. They also determined which department heads could have county cars, what those cars would be, and what the financial policy regarding take-home cars would be. The federal Family Medical Leave Act (FMLA) was passed after I became auditor and the commissioners are the ones who had to approve each request for family leave.

They hired the firm that handled our job classification and approved or disapproved the recommendations made by the job classification committee. They made appointments to many various boards and councils throughout the county, and sometimes served on some of those boards or councils themselves. It was their job to oversee the construction and/or maintenance of every county-owned building. They had to maintain it, insure it, and make sure it met the federal handicap requirements. The federal disability act was passed during my second year as auditor, so there was a lot to do to bring some of the older buildings up to handicap codes. It was their job to approve the election precinct polling places and make sure they met handicap standards, also.

Another huge area of responsibility was the county highway department, which of course included construction and maintenance of all of the county's roads. The highway department is responsible for 911 miles of roads and 114 bridges. They also maintain culverts and curbs, and of course keep the roads cleared during the winter snow season. Taking care of all those roads and bridges requires an enormous amount of equipment, storage for salt, and road improvement supplies, a maintenance garage to maintain all those trucks and equipment, and on and on. This department was always close to the hearts of most of the commissioners. They worked very closely with the highway supervisor and his key employees, and kept pretty good track of what was happening out there.

In Indiana, if a county hired an engineer, the state would supplement part of their salary. You would think, with two of the country's premier engineering schools in the state, Purdue and Rose Hullman, it would be easy to find someone. Not so much. At that time, the highway supervisor was a man who had worked his way up through the ranks, and was not a trained engineer. They did hire an engineer near the end of my term as auditor, but he didn't really work out very well, so they let him go and put the other fellow back in that position.

The highway department was one of the most controversial areas of county government. Citizens drove on county roads and if they didn't think they were in good enough shape, then the commissioners heard about it. People were always complaining about the lack of tax dollars being spent on the roads, and they were right. Indiana law did not allow for property tax dollars to be spent on county roads. Road funding comes from fuel taxes, license and registration fees, and some optional programs, such as wheel taxes, determined by the county. At the time I left office, Marshall County had not opted for those additional funding sources, and there may have been many changes since then, but there is still no property tax funds going to roads. Generally, citizens who pay those property taxes, just don't understand that; so they continually fuss at the commissioners to 'fix their roads.' The Commissioners and highway supervisor do the best they can with the funds available to them.

Every year in March, Purdue University would host a school for county commissioners, highway supervisors, and auditors. Except for the auditor's portion of the meeting, this school, affectionately known as 'road school', was a giant testosterone festival. In my day, there were only a few female commissioners, and I can't remember any female highway supervisors, but most of the auditors were female. There were of course, many different sessions, and we could attend any that we chose. In addition to our auditor's session, I often attended anything that had to do with the funding portion. Otherwise, I found other things to do. Even the hospitality rooms didn't have much appeal, just too much boy stuff.

One of the highlights of road school was a wonderful dinner hosted by the engineering company we worked with. The county had a contract with this company and we had gotten to know their engineer very well. The contracted project was a major plan to build a completely new connector road from the south side of Plymouth to State Road 17, on the west side near the new hospital. The connector started from Oakhill Avenue in Plymouth and was called the Oakhill Avenue project. Because the connector was going to traverse wet lands, it was an environmental nightmare and took a real pro to dig through the obstacles with the Army Corps of Engineers. This fellow was the perfect choice. Needless to say, after nearly twenty years of trying to complete this project, the commissioners, the auditor, the engineer, and the woman who handled business development for their company, all became very good friends. I got to know them as I traveled around the state with Mary B during my holdover year, then of course as I took over the helm as auditor and they continued to work on the project. As mentioned in chapter four, this is the project that I convinced Mary B to come and join us for the ribbon cutting—she had worked on it much longer than I did.

Every year at road school, this company would invite the commissioners, highway supervisors, auditors, and anyone else attending from their customer counties. The dinner was held at a famous seafood restaurant in Lafayette, home to Purdue, and featured an all you can eat seafood buffet that was to die for. It also included an open bar. Since they represented many counties throughout Indiana, there were always lots of people I knew besides the folks from Marshall County. Unfortunately, I only got to attend a few of those dinners before the restaurant was destroyed in a fire. The company tried to replicate it at a couple of other places in town, but it was just never the same and eventually they gave it up. We worked hard as county officials, so once in a while the perks were a very special treat and worth all of that hard work.

During my eight years as auditor I worked with nine different county commissioners. Some I got to know better than others; a couple I knew before they took office; and all but one of them were members of my political party. Ironically, the one who wasn't, was the best commissioner I ever worked with. He was smart, funny, cared only about what was best for the citizens, and wasn't intimidated by anyone. Unfortunately, that included our sheriff. This commissioner had served as Marshall County Sheriff in the sixties, so he was well aware of what that job was all about. Even with many changes over the years, and he acknowledged those changes, he still thought the sheriff tried to take advantage of the county. He was right. But because everyone in office was of the same party, nobody had ever taken on the sheriff. When I started as clerk, the sheriff and I got along okay; I considered him a friend. But after I was in office a while, I figured out his program and the relationship went downhill pretty fast. So I was delighted to have a commissioner who finally saw what was going on with the sheriff and was willing to try and stop some of it.

For example, Marshall County, with the population of about 45,000 people at that time, owned a helicopter. I don't know why we owned a helicopter, nor when or where we got the helicopter. I know that there were only two helicopter pilots (both flew helicopters in Viet Nam) in the entire county. One of them was a deputy sheriff, so the helicopter was under the purview of the sheriff's office. Everyone knows that all pilots have to fly so many hours to keep their license, so the big joke was when the helicopter flew over, the pilot must be going somewhere for dinner. Marshall County did not really need a helicopter. And, to make matters worse, this was our second one. The deputy had crashed the first one. Well, something happened to this helicopter, I don't remember if it was crashed again, or just mechanical problems, but it was going to cost a lot of money to fix it and make it airborne again. And two of the commissioners did not want to spend the money on it. Twenty-five miles away from Plymouth was a state police garage that housed two state police helicopters. They were called in during emergencies if someone needed to be air lifted to a hospital or a search of some sort was necessary. Again, nobody really knew why Marshall County owned their own helicopter. So, after their research, and discussion, pleading, and begging by the two pilots and the sheriff, their attempts to justify the expense for the helicopter; (insurance, gas, maintenance, not to mention current repairs), the commissioners voted not to repair the helicopter, and found a buyer for it, as it was. That was not an easy decision, but given that most folks knew we didn't need it, and other county officials around the state thought it was hysterical that we had a helicopter, for crying out loud. It turned out to be a pretty good decision. And it was the Democrat who started what none of the Republicans over the years had the guts to do.

I had always been very proud of my record, as an officeholder, of not ever having been sued until the end of my seventh year as auditor. Damn it. Guess who? The sheriff's office. Apparently, some of the sheriff's deputies decided that the sheriff was playing games with the hours that the deputies worked. They maintained that they were not being paid everything they were owed, because he was trying to stay within his budget and not have to ask for more money. That is a worthy goal, but not at the expense of your employees. So they filed suit against the sheriff, but also against the commissioners, the county council, and the auditor. Well, that was just ridiculous. Sue the sheriff if you want, but leave the rest of us out of it. The county council sets the salary, but that's all they have to do with payroll. The county commissioners approve the payroll based on what I published, but that is all they have to do with payroll. The county auditor 'audits' the payroll—i.e., is the employee listed an actual employee? And are the employees listed being paid the amount in the salary ordinance? Is there enough money in the line item for payroll to meet that need? That is all the auditor has to do with payroll. The auditor does not take attendance, and the sheriff (or his authorized representative) signed the payroll form that it was correct, under penalties of perjury. The auditor can't arbitrarily change it. So sue the sheriff, not everybody else!

I found out about this lawsuit on the last day of the county commissioner's annual meeting in Indianapolis. One of them came to my room as we were getting ready to leave and showed me the petition for the lawsuit. I told him right then and there it was crap as far as the commissioners, me, and the council goes, but I was not going to have the county attorney represent me. If they wanted him fine, but I was hiring an expert in personnel matters and they were going to pay for it. Well, this particular commissioner agreed with me, and during the drive home we convinced the other two. I had met just the right lawyer at the previous Association of Indiana Counties annual meeting. He spoke at a seminar on personnel issues. He was from Ft. Wayne and I agreed to call him when I got back to the office and schedule him to attend a commissioners' meeting. We also called an executive meeting (no press) with the county council when we got back, to discuss the lawsuit. At that meeting, everyone but one council person agreed we needed an expert lawyer.

When it came time to discuss this in public, one commissioner lost his nerve and would not vote against the county attorney who was sitting there (I never trusted that commissioner again) but the other two hung tough and we were able to hire the expert. Over the next several months (litigation moves at a snail's pace) our attorney took depositions and responded to the various filings of the deputies' lawyer. The plaintiff's attorney had subpoenaed several years worth of payroll records from my office, and getting those together would have taken hours for my staff. Our attorney said I didn't have to pull individual files, just make them available. So the day he was to come in and get those records, we put all of the files drawers on a table in the office, where everyone could see him, and said 'help yourself.' We showed him where the copy machine was and reminded him that the county charged a dollar a page for copies. He was livid. He said that he had expected to have all of that ready for him at no charge. I told him that we were in compliance with the subpoena, so if he wanted copies, he had to do it himself, and nowhere did it say I had to provide those copies free of charge. He was angry, but he left and never bothered me or my staff again. The case was still open when I left office, but I did hear later that the commissioners, council, and auditor were all dismissed from the complaint and the sheriff was ordered to pay the deputies back pay. None of us were surprised by the ruling, we all knew that the sheriff played games with employee hours. Of course, the county had to pay it, but at least my lawsuit-free record was intact, not something that happens very often.

The job of County Commissioner is really quite involved and can be complicated. One of the people they worked the closest with, besides the auditor, was the county attorney. He was on a retainer to attend all of the commissioners meetings, and then was paid hourly for any other work he did for the county. I'm not sure the commissioners truly understood that, because they had him do some jobs that we had plenty of staff capable of handling at no extra cost. For example, a new telephone system was needed in the county building. After the bidding was over and a company was hired, instead of having me or someone else in the building go around and do an 'inventory' of what was needed in each office, they sent the attorney, at the attorney's hourly prices!

Unfortunately from my experience as clerk, I didn't have a very good working relationship with the county attorney when I moved to the auditor's office. He was another one who new I would be 'hands on' and watch what was happening very closely. He liked my organizational skills, he never had to ask me twice for information, but he was a terrible procrastinator and his answer was always, "I'll take care of that next time," and he never came through. After I saw the first bill he turned into the county, we went to war. He only turned in bills, twice a year. That is impossible to audit. He had been doing that for a very long time and Mary B didn't seem to mind. But my claims deputy came to me not long after I started and asked me if we could have him submit monthly bills like everyone else. So I requested he do that, he agreed, then totally ignored my request and did nothing. This happened several more times. Then my deputy came back to me concerned that the county attorney had charged us twice for over $1000.00. She asked me to look at it. I did, and determined that she was right. I knew his secretary, and I knew she would not have done that on purpose, but with only billing twice a year, it was easy to make the mistake. Now I had my ammunition when I took it to the commissioners, in a public meeting, and politely requested that the county attorney be directed to submit a monthly bill like all of our other regular vendors. I gave the board copies of the two bills, and that is when they realized how much he was charging the county for every single thing. Many of the department heads and elected officials were under the misconception that there was one contract for everything. They didn't realize it was just a retainer to attend commissioner meetings. Department heads thought nothing of picking up the phone to get some legal advice, having no idea each and every instance was being billed separately. The commissioners were flabbergasted when I explained that to them. Right then they made the decision that no department head could call the attorney without bringing it before them first, so they would decide if it was necessary to incur the expense. I told the board that I had previously asked the attorney for monthly bills. When I pointed out all of the problems that can arise, billing us twice for the same thing for over $1000, the board agreed, made and passed a motion requiring monthly billing. The attorney had no choice and he was so angry that his face was flaming red. I thought he was going to explode. He hated me from that point on. I cost him a lot of money. But I didn't care, right is right and it was taxpayer money. He was taking advantage of his position, and of the auditor's office—but not this auditor. Additional problems arose over the next few years as different people became commissioners, and eventually that attorney resigned. I had a wonderful working relationship with the new county attorney, and it never even occurred to him to not bill the county monthly. He did a great job and I think he is still serving in that capacity.

I know the commissioners often had to make very difficult decisions. There was no way they could please everyone, and for the most part they did their best to make sure their decisions were based on what was best for the county. I served with nine commissioners during my eight years as auditor. I got along with seven of them really, really well. I got along with the other two, sometimes. Unfortunately these two had a less than modern attitude toward women. Shall we say they really didn't care for a strong woman who would speak her mind? Me, you say? On occasion.

Most of the time, when a new commissioner came in, they soon realized that I had a pretty good handle on the job and county government in general, and would come to me with their questions, concerns, etc. I was always happy to help. Lots of people had helped me when I was new. But one time that just didn't happen with a new commissioner. As a matter of fact, he sent letters to many of the state boards and groups we worked with, and asked all kinds of questions that could easily have been answered by many of our own department heads. By that time, I knew just about everyone at those state offices who dealt with county officials, and they started calling me. They would tell me that they got this strange letter from a guy in Marshall County and they didn't know what to do with it. When they told me who it was, I laughed, explained the situation, and told them to throw it away. Later, when I would see them in person, I asked many of them if they had ever heard from him again, they all said no. After they met him in person, most of them came and told me they understood why I suggested they throw away the letters! What a hoot.

On my last day in office, this particular commissioner asked if he could speak to me in my office. There wasn't much left in my office, I had been cleaning it out for weeks. I also thought it was a bit late to come and start asking me questions, but I said sure. Turns out, he just want to tell me how sorry he was about my husband's illness, he and his wife had always liked Tom. I said thank you, and he turned and walked away. Always liked Tom. Apparently didn't like me, just Tom. Again, what a hoot.

There were many times that I was frustrated with the commissioners because I thought they backed away from some of the harder situations and let people get away with things because it was just easier. One year in October, I told my staff I was going to buy three of those dangling Halloween skeletons, take them apart, and put the backbone at each place on the commissioner's table and tell them, "This is what a spine looks like." My staff wouldn't let me. But brother, for someone like me, seeing them back down could be pretty hard to watch.

The Indiana Association of County Commissioners

This group is the affiliate association for county commissioners. Because the auditor works so closely with the commissioners, we are invited to all of their meetings and conferences. The IACC is divided into the same districts as the AIC and again, we were in the Northwest District. They met on a regular basis and I usually went with them to the meetings. They often 'expanded' their meetings to include golf outings in the afternoon. Golf always included vendors, who frequently paid the green fees, bought lunch, etc. As one of a few lady golfers in the group, I was always invited to go and spend the entire afternoon and evening at the meetings, but I was usually too busy at the office for the golf. When I was able to spare the time I rarely teamed up with my own commissioners. I generally played as a guest of a female vendor who I knew well. Since I worked all summer and my golf time was limited, I really enjoyed those opportunities to play at various golf courses in our district. However, it was not easy transitioning from golf mode, (casual clothes, all hot and sweaty), to dinner mode, (professional clothes, hair and makeup), in a tiny little restroom shared by the other gals who were also trying to transition. Could be quite the challenge.

One of the IACC meetings I liked best was the commissioners annual meeting. It always took place at the Indianapolis Sheraton

Hotel at Keystone Crossing, which had a walkway to a fashion mall. You didn't even have to go outside to go shopping!!

The auditors had a meeting of their own and it was the last one of the year. We did a wrap-up of the year, talked about settlement and end of the year responsibilities, and usually tried to sneak in some Christmas shopping. We also were invited to any of the commissioners sessions and I did go to the ones that interested me most. The vendors were set up in the grand hall, trade-show style, like they did at the AIC conference, so it was fun to hang out there, see their wares, and chat with my vendor friends.

The hospitality rooms at the IACC were the same as Road School—testosterone festivals—so I rarely hung out in those rooms in the evening. Sometimes, a specific vendor would ask a few auditors to dinner or drinks, and we would go for that. A lot more fun than watching the vendors try to impress the commissioners through lots of drinking, playing cards, cussing, and telling dirty jokes. Fortunately my commissioners were not like that, but many of the boy vendors were, especially those who handled road and engineering stuff.

Over the years, I learned how to get my way with the guys, sometimes without them even knowing it. We clashed on occasion, but for the most part, there was a great deal of mutual respect. Overall, I found working with the commissioners interesting, informative, and generally fun. I'll always remember my 'boys' with fondness.

Chapter 14
The Money Managers

In Indiana, there is another governing county body—the County Council. This is a group of seven elected officials, four from specific districts and three at large. They are the fiscal body. They handle all funding requests through the budget procedure, including the commissioners' budget. I was the fiscal officer of the county so my job was to work with the council in helping develop the budget, and provide all of the necessary information they would need to make their decisions. The council met once a month, except during the budget hearings, which were in the summer and usually lasted two or three days.

A huge part of the budgeting process was gathering information from other department heads and elected officials by the July first deadline. Hopefully before that date, the council would have agreed on a number or percentage range for pay raises for the next year to guide the department heads and officeholders to give them a chance to build those raises into their budget. Most used the numbers supplied by the council, but a few did not and asked for more. That never worked. After they turned their budget requests into me, I would compile all of them into one large 'county budget' request and give the requests to the council members to study. At the beginning of the year, each council member had been assigned as liaisons to certain departments. Their job was to meet with those department heads and discuss their budget request—some did, some didn't.

During the month of July, I would then pull together all of the figures I could get concerning the county revenue. What came from taxes, and what was considered 'miscellaneous revenue' (i.e., all non-tax dollar revenues collected for other purposes). For example: building department fees, state and county portions of court costs, health department fees, etc.

Then I compiled all of the numbers: the total budget requests, the revenue estimate, and any other information that goes into developing a tax rate. I put that in a packet for the council members to pick up and study before the budget hearings. Only a few ever did. Then in August, we would have a two-day meeting that gave the council the opportunity to meet with every officeholder and department head to discuss that person's budget request, and make any changes that they agreed on.

Immediately after Labor Day, the council would meet again, armed with the financial information that I had given them (some looked at it, some didn't) and began to make final decisions on each department budget. The commissioners' budget was one of the hardest because it included things like insurance for county employees, payroll taxes for the entire county, and more.

Before the council could ever act on the budgets, all of the information had to be published as a legal newspaper advertisement.

That gave the public plenty of time to see what was being asked for and, if they wanted to attend the meeting and ask questions, they could. Everything about the process was public information.

After the council concluded their work and made their decisions on salaries and individual budgets, it was my job to again compile all of that information for the individual departments; put together a salary ordinance outlining each position in the county and what it would pay the next year; advertise the final budget; and send everything out to the departments. But there was a big caveat—please don't shoot the messenger!! Overall, I enjoyed pulling the budget together, although I could have done without the advertising deadlines.

I thought (and still do) that the best way to budget is to over-estimate expenditures and under-estimate revenue; then you are usually pretty safe. Also, there were mechanisms built into the system for additional appropriations. If a department ran out of money, or needed more in a different area, they could make a request to the council throughout the year. After those requests were advertised according to statute, the council could act on them. After all, a budget is a guess, and things come up that nobody can foresee, so those kinds of requests took place throughout the year and the council did the best they could for everyone. Part of my responsibility was to make sure that there were enough unappropriated funds in the budget to allow for these requests. Throughout my entire eight years as auditor I made the same recommendation to council; do not let the unappropriated funds (somewhat like a savings account) get below one million dollars. I had hoped they would pass a resolution for that but they never did. It came close to going under that amount while I was in office, but never dipped below it. That did happen in later years, and I was sorry that they had not put something in writing to avoid that. But I could only make the suggestion, I couldn't make it happen.

The Money Managers

The members of the County Council were all part time and only met once a month, except for the budget hearings. Unless they had served in another office, they weren't all that well acquainted with the various departments and what they did. I personally thought the budget and finances were some of the most important parts of county government administration. But I have to say, I was amazed at some of the things I heard and saw over the years. For example:

- One time the coroner was discussing his budget request and had asked for a new vehicle. He was currently using an old one from the sheriff's office and it was beginning to need too much repair work. He stated that he would be fine with another used car, but he really did need a station wagon or van for transporting bodies for autopsy to South Bend. (We did not have facilities in Marshall County.) Pretty reasonable request. Then one of the council members asked him if the bodies that were transported were dead. Well, there was little bit of silence then everyone started laughing. I nudged the chairman sitting next to me and asked him to promise that, if I was being hauled to autopsy, he would make sure I was dead.
- Another time we were all gathered around the conference table getting ready to begin, and a member of the council said, "I don't know how we can make these spending decisions when we don't have any idea what the revenue will be." After the steam came out of my ears, I proceeded to point him to the sheet ON THE TOP OF THE PILE that had all of the revenue figures on it. Obviously, he did not do his homework.
- I was always amazed at how quickly the council members who had previously served as full-time elected officials with their own departments and budgets, could forget that they had once been in the same situation but now didn't seem to want anyone to have any money. I respect that it is public funds, but really, people deserved decent pay and decent benefits, and council

members sometimes overlooked that basic decency when trying to 'save the public money.'

- I will never forget the budget hearing I attended while I was clerk. When they began discussing employee raises, one male member of the council suggested that the county only give raises to the men, and to females who were not married!! He said, "Since the married employees have husbands to take care of them they didn't need as much money." Holy smokes. I about fell off my chair. Fortunately, the other six members jumped right on that and reminded him that we would spend more money defending discrimination lawsuits than we would save. Not to mention, an employee is an employee; their marital status had nothing to do with their salary.

- One of the best council members to ever serve during my term was also a banker. The county finances with all of the zeroes didn't intimidate him like it did some of the others. Also, because he ran a business, he understood employee concerns and how to treat them. He was the only one who always came to my office and went over budget information with me so that, by the time the hearings came around, he was the most prepared. Unfortunately he was a Democrat in a highly Republican county and when redistricting was done, the Republican commissioners eliminated his district so he would have to run against a Republican. He did, and lost. It was a huge loss to the county and the citizens, but I guess a win for the GOP. How you see it depends on what matters most, the citizens or the party. I always picked the citizens, but I was only one vote.

I generally enjoyed working with the council. Some of them upset me because I didn't feel like they did their homework or really made an effort to understand county finances. I get that—they only met once a month, except for the budget hearings, and over the years, most of them were busy in other areas. None of them did it for the money, (the pay was a pittance), but they did have access to the county insurance, so that was a plus for them. Like all governments, some of the council members were outstanding public servants and a joy to work with, some others, not so much.

State Tax Board
(Now the Indiana Department of Local Government Finance)

Within a few years after I left office, the name of the State Tax Board was changed, but I think the basic duties were the same. Our involvement with the tax board was primarily the budgeting process and all things having to do with tax assessments. I have already explained the budgeting, but even though the auditor's office had nothing to do with tax collection, we maintained all of the property records in the state and, of course, the assessed valuation is determined by the value of each parcel of property.

I did not have a close working relationship with the people at this state agency like I did some of the other boards, although I always attended their meetings. Their state representatives also participated in the SBA state-called meetings. However, they did have field agents who were assigned 'territories.' In other words, a few counties around where they lived. My first state tax rep lived in neighboring Starke County, and he worked out of Marshall County almost every day. We had an empty desk right outside of my office door, and that is where he worked. I liked him a lot; he was very knowledgeable, very helpful, and personable. He answered many of my questions and was a wonderful guy to have around, especially during my first couple years in office.

Eventually he moved on, and then the second field rep to work out of my office was really special. It was a man I had known all of my life. He was a Rochester native, like me, and grew up right down the street from where I lived. He was two years behind me in high school (a pretty small school), so we had a wonderful time working together, sharing stories, catching up on all the people and events we both knew. He lived in South Bend, but like me, never forgot his Rochester roots, so having him there was really special. In fact, one day I stopped at his desk to ask if he knew that the former Rochester football coach, (who was teaching there when he and I were students) had been killed. This coach had lived right next door to him, and I used to babysit for the coach's kids. We had both liked the coach very much, and we ended up chatting about him and other teachers for at least two hours. It was sometimes difficult to maintain our 'professional' working relationship since we had such a strong history, especially with my tendency to want to call him by his high school nickname, "Spike", instead of his real name, "Mike." But he always responded to whichever name I used!

Since we moved to Marshall County in 1971, there has been a combination of men and women serve on the County Council, but we have only had one female commissioner and the two male commissioners ran her out. I don't believe there has been another woman elected as commissioner since I left. Have to wonder if Marshall County's citizens don't think the boys can handle the money by themselves. Have to wonder....

Chapter 15
Pay the People, Pay the Bills, Pay the Political Sub-divisions

Another large part of the auditor's duties was paying the bills. We handled all of the payroll for the county, as well as the HR duties that went along with that. We also paid the general bills, and disbursed the funds to all of the political sub-divisions twice a year.

Pay the People

I was always amazed by how many county employees did not think the rules applied to them—except my payroll deputy. Remember that election deputy I mentioned earlier, the one that stayed with me for my entire sixteen years? She was my payroll deputy in the auditor's office. And she followed the book. Payroll was governed by three 'bibles'—the salary ordinance signed by the county council; state and federal payroll statutes; and the county employee handbook. And those are the references she used in auditing every department's payroll. Did they follow the salary ordinance? If they granted sick or vacation days, was it within the guidelines of the county employee manual? Were the state and federal statutes followed, especially for newly enrolled employees?

We were required by law to advertise every single, solitary payroll the county approved. We were paid every other week, that is twenty-six paydays, twenty-six legal ads. Legal ads have deadlines; we couldn't wait until someone 'remembered' that it was payroll day. People can be pretty flexible sometimes, but not when it came to their paycheck.

What many of the employees never seemed to understand, was we paid them based on information given to us by their department head. The county council set the salaries in an ordinance and we had to follow it. But it only outlined the approved pay rate; not the hours the employee actually worked. The hours of the departments was set by the commissioners. Also all employees, except department heads and elected officials were hourly, so when their department head said they had worked a certain number of hours, those were the hours we paid for. When my deputy would question the amount of hours, usually because they seemed excessive for a particular position, I reminded her it was not our job to take attendance. The payroll claim forms were signed by the head of the department, under penalties of perjury. If they lied, that was 'ghost employment' and they could go to jail. On the few occasions when that happened, I brought it to the attention of the commissioners and they could check it out if they wanted. They generally did.

Both the council members and the commissioners hated overtime pay; with some exceptions for the highway department and the sheriff's department. They preferred that any extra hours that were needed be paid through 'compensatory time'. Now comp time is fine, but they didn't seem to understand that comp time was also 'paid' at time and a half. If you worked an extra three hours, you were supposed to get four and one half hours off.

Very few department heads did that. They generally allowed comp time on an hour-for-hour basis and their employees seemed okay with that, or more likely didn't know the difference. None of the offices were overstaffed, so when someone is gone, it makes it harder for everyone else. Comp time is time off, so that office is short staffed, therefore not everyone was able to take their comp time. The problem with that was, if they let the comp time accrue, then when they left the position, they needed to be paid for that time. That is fine, except if too much time went by, an employee could earn it at one rate, and expect to be paid at their current rate, which might be considerably higher, depending on the amount of time that had passed. Well, that really screws up a budget, so the commissioners finally set a limit on how long an employee could 'hold' their accrued comp time. After that time, they were required to use it, or get paid for it, or lose it. Period.

I found it very interesting that many employees really didn't pay much attention to what was happening with payroll. We would have experts come in and talk to them about the various benefits the county offered, how they worked, and what was expected of the employee. Every employee was expected to attend those meetings, and had to sign in. We had several meetings, always during work hours, so no department had to close. They just had to divide up their staff to attend different meetings. And yet, invariably someone would come along later and feign complete ignorance regarding something that happened with their paycheck, or regarding their benefits.. For example:

- One time, an employee from another department called my payroll deputy and raised all kinds of hell because he decided that she had taken some money out of his check that he did not authorize. I believe it was for some extra insurance. When she told him that she had been doing that all along, he told her that was wrong and she had no right to do it. He told her he was coming right over to take care of it. By the time he arrived in our office, she had pulled the authorization sheet for that particular withholding, signed by him, and dated over two years previously. To say the least, he was a bit embarrassed.

- Another time, an employee was having some health issues, and she ran out of sick days. Her boss was so scared of her that he decided she could 'work from home.' We didn't have a work from home policy, and in those days we didn't have the means (internet) to allow working from home. We ended up having to get the commissioners to declare that 'work from home' was not authorized and would not be paid.

- There was also a certain percentage of employees who wasted their sick days. Sick days are not a benefit; our policy allowed employees to accrue one half day each month up to a total of thirty-six days. Once you had thirty-six days days, you stopped accruing until you used one. For most folks that was fine. But some took a sick day every month, usually at the beginning of the month when they earned a new one. Then, when they really got sick with something that required several days off, they would yell and scream because they had to take time without pay or vacation time (because they had already used their days) just like it said in the employee handbook.

- One day, a department head came in and sat down and said he had an employee who failed the drug test. What should he do? I said, "The young man would need to be terminated." The boss said, "I don't want to do that, his father also works for me and will be mad." I responded, "too bad, the kid broke the rules, he has to be terminated; his dad will need to get over it, or quit."

- Of course, we had one department, the sheriff's office, that worked 24/7, but our office was not open 24/7. So, one payroll period they turned in their payroll and there is a name that my deputy has never heard of. When she called them to ask about it, she was told it was a new employee who had never come in to get signed up for payroll. WELL WE CAN'T PAY SOMEBODY WE DON'T KNOW ABOUT for crying out loud. Turns out the new employee worked third shift and just didn't get around to coming in while we were in the office. My answer, "Okay, but we can't get around to paying anyone without paperwork." He came in the next day.

- When I first started as auditor, we discovered that the sheriff's office had been signing second and third shift people up for payroll in their offices, when they worked, and not sending them to our office. When I heard that I went bat-shit crazy and said no, no, no, never again. Talk about setting yourself up for ghost employment, not to mention the federal form that we have to sign that we have ACTUALLY SEEN their documentation that gives them the right to work in America. Yeah, we won't be doing that anywhere but in the auditor's office. I understood that many of their employees worked second and third shift. But that meant they were available to come into the auditor's office and sign up during the day. That was the only way they were going to be paid—not negotiable. It was only one trip, and they probably earned comp time for coming in their off hours. They all seemed to make it from then on.

The Auditor's office was located in the county building, that had been built in the mid-seventies. It was relatively modern and very nice. Unfortunately, the office was one great big open room, except for the small conference room that I had commandeered for my office. I was very uncomfortable that the payroll deputy sat out right in the middle of things. Since she also handled HR issues, insurance, benefits, sick days, vacation questions, etc, I felt that she should have some privacy. That would show a bit more respect to county employees when they had a need to come and see her. I went searching throughout the building and found a couple of old cubicle walls that were not being used. I moved her to a corner of the room, so that only one side of her 'office' faced out; where the employees could sit with their back to the room. I think that made people more comfortable when discussing such personal matters. Well, it wasn't long until some of my other employees were asking for 'private' offices so they would have less distractions. I tried to accommodate the best I could, but we still had an obligation to watch the front desk, answer the phone, and take care of the public. If you are behind walls, you can't effectively do that. After I left the auditor's office, apparently my successor put up walls around all of the deputies. The commissioners had so many complaints that they ordered him to take them all down, including the payroll office. I always thought removing the privacy for human resources was a real shame. I think since then the HR office has been moved into the old commissioner's office, so it is totally private. That was probably a pretty good move.

Many times I've thought that every single employee, department head, or other official of any kind of business should have to do payroll for at least six months. I think they would really have their eyes opened as to how difficult it really is. And yes, I know it was automated, we had payroll software that did the math, but all the data still had to be entered correctly. Almost all of the counties in Indiana, except probably the largest ones, handled their own payroll. I looked into payroll services from time to time, but they really were very expensive back them. The commissioners just didn't want it to go 'out of house' so we did the best we could. My deputy and I went to all of the payroll/HR seminars and workshops that were available and tried to stay up to date on the various law and statute changes, but it wasn't always easy.

However, those extra 'classes' served me well on one occasion. Our county had a policy that some of the department heads or elected officials could have 'take home' cars. Now, those cars were not anything fancy, and often came from departments that were upgrading their vehicles. However, each person was charged three dollars a day for the use of the vehicle, as supplementary income. That is not a bad cost when you consider that it included all of the maintenance, (done by the highway department) gas, insurance, and any other costs, all paid by the county. Then that amount was added to their W-2 at the end of the year and they had to pay income taxes on those funds. Well, one year the commissioners decided they did not like having to pay taxes on the extra income. So they wrote an ordinance that said they didn't have to. The county attorney wrote the ordinance, which meant he was okay with it. I was blown away. Income taxes are governed by federal payroll law, not by county ordinance. When I pointed that out to them, they objected and told me that since the attorney said it was okay, that is the way they were going to do it.

So, in Mary Lou style, before the next meeting, I did lots and lots of research, and found the exact federal law that listed the extra money as income and required that it be taxed. When I presented it to them at a meeting, with the attorney present, I told them if they wanted to defy federal law, they had to put it in writing and sign it. Because, if there is a problem with federal funds, the feds will put a lien on my personal bank account, not the county. So, they needed to pick a person responsible, because there was not going to be a lean on the Tom and Mary Lou checkbook just so they didn't have to pay taxes on their extra income. Of course I didn't care who else ended up with a lien on behalf of the county. They rescinded the ordinance and paid the taxes. And that, my friends, is why they call it 'auditing' the books.

Pay the Bills

We also paid all of the county's bills, known as 'claims.' My job as auditor, and the deputies who did those specific jobs, was to make sure that all of the bills were paid in accordance to statute, ordinance, and of course the council approved budgets. We not only had to make sure that the money was in their budget, but make sure the bills were paid from the correct funds. For example, you can't pay a bill for copy paper from the payroll funds. So, every single bill being paid from county funds, regardless of where they came from, had to go through the auditors office. And of course, those claims had to be advertised in the paper for a certain number of days before the commissioners' meeting, because although the commissioners didn't set the budget, but they had to approve all expenditures. I couldn't release the checks until the board approved. It was usually a 'rubber stamp' type approval unless something really jumped out at them. If that did occur, we did our best to catch it before the meeting, so the appropriate commissioner would have time to visit with the office holder or department head and get more information. We didn't catch them all, but we tried.

The claims portion of the auditor's office was basically the same each month. The commissioners didn't micro manage the way each officeholder or department head spent their money. They probably figured that was my job, but they did have some rules. Anything out of the ordinary that cost more than $100 required their approval. And although the IV-D funds that the clerk and prosecutor had didn't require spending approval, most of the things they wanted to buy exceeded the $100 threshold, so they did need approval for that item. One of the more interesting requests for the use of IV-D funds was by my successor in the clerk's office. He wanted to buy a couch for his private office. When the commissioners asked why he needed a couch he said that sometimes he got really tired on long election days and it would be nice to rest. Also, he sometimes had deputies or staff that didn't feel well and they would want to lie down. Well, needless to say, since I was in the room taking minutes, I didn't know whether to laugh or scream. The county attorney asked me if I had ever slept during a long election day and of course I told him no, because I didn't. If my staff ever felt ill, I made them go home and take a sick day. There's no sleeping in the office on county time. Lordy. Of course, they approved his purchase, and I remember going over to the clerk's office after that for something, and being told to be quiet, one of the deputies had a headache and was resting on the couch. I very loudly said no, I won't be quiet, this is a workplace, not a sick bay. Shortly after that she got up and went back to her desk.

The biggest problem we ever had processing claims was getting them turned in on time. Of course, they had to be advertised so many days before the commissioners' meeting which creates a deadline. I know people get busy and forget, and I didn't mind if my deputy reminded them once in a while, but having to badger someone to turn in their required paperwork every month was unacceptable. She shouldn't have to beg and cajole someone to do their job.

One of the things I handled was 'obligating' funds. At the end of the year, if you had an outstanding bill and wanted it to be paid from the current year's budget, but the bill would not be paid until January, there was a procedure for using current year's money. They had to use a state form, and attach the bill to the form. Then I could pay the bill from the previous year's funds and not take away from their new budget. Again, the biggest problem was they had to be turned in by December 31 and it took several reminders for people to get that done.

The deputy who paid the bills, also kept track of the vendors who required 1099s for taxes. Many of the bills went to regular businesses or utilities, or whatever. But since we also paid bills for the townships, we often had folks who collected rent or were self-employed. It was also her job to make sure that everyone who was to get a 1099 tax form actually received one. Getting those vendors to fill out the W-9 forms was sometimes impossible. I finally instituted a procedure, the first time we paid a bill for someone in that situation, they had to come in and fill out the W-9 and then they could pick up their check. Once we had the completed, signed form, we were happy to put their subsequent checks in the mail. They didn't like it very well, but it worked.

Paying the county's bills was a never-ending job of course, just like paying household bills. But during my terms as auditor, I was lucky to have three top notch claims deputies. The first one I inherited and she stayed and worked for me until she retired. The second one worked that desk until her husband was transferred and they moved out of state. The third one was still there when I left, and continued for several more years. All three of them were great ladies, fun to work with, and really knew their stuff. Learning the claims process is not easy, but after they were trained that was one desk I never really worried about. If there was a question or problem, they brought it to me. Otherwise, I just left them to it as they quietly paid the counties bills.

Pay the Political Sub-divisions

Political sub-divisions are also known as schools, libraries, cities, towns, and townships. Indiana law requires that the auditor distribute all of the funds that are collected (generally property tax funds), to each of these entities twice a year. It is called settlement—settling up with them—and the statute says it must be done by June 30 and December 31. The June 30 deadline is for the entities that have a July-June fiscal year. Most bond payments are due July 1, so they need their funds in time to pay those bills. Of course, December 31 is the end of the other fiscal years (not including Federal, they are October 1 through September 30). The first one in June was not quite as difficult as the one in December.

The final settlement included some items that were only disbursed once a year, and was also a chance to reconcile the first settlement and anything we might have missed. Of course, taxes can't be disbursed if the taxes aren't collected, so that was often a factor also. Settlement is a really big job, done in a rather small amount of time, from the last day to pay taxes (May 10 and November 10) until the deadlines of June 30 and December 31. The auditor can't start settlement until the treasurer (who collects the taxes) has balanced her collections and turned the information over to my office. From that point on, my settlement deputy does nothing else.

One of the reasons that the auditor has the responsibility to distribute the funds is because we are custodians of all of the property records in the county. We keep track of ownership of the property; if there are any liens on the property; if there are any deductions; any exemptions; anything at all that has to do with a parcel of land or personal property. Since settlement is based on each parcel, it's assessed valuation, it's tax liability and what is collected, it makes sense that it is done in the auditor's office.

When I began my first term as auditor, the settlement deputy also served as the payroll deputy. Whew—talk about a lot to do. I soon decided that was too much responsibility for one person, so I eventually decided to divide the job between two people. Later, when we began using new payroll software, I moved payroll to another deputy. The former payroll deputy didn't have to learn the new software and the new payroll deputy didn't have to learn the old software, just the mechanics of the job in general. Since I was a hands-on officeholder, I worked on the new software, adding all of the parameter information, account numbers, names, and other information getting it set up and ready to use. That is a great way to learn new software, believe me. Not long after I made the decision to split the job, my payroll/settlement deputy announced that she was retiring from the county and moving out of state. I don't believe she cared much for my decision.

She had been in the auditor's office for many, many years, so I asked her who she thought would be the best person to train. One deputy in particular had expressed an interest in doing that job, so the outgoing deputy assured me the interested deputy could do it and would train her. I took her at her word and moved the other gal over. They worked together for a long time, and I kept asking how the new gal was doing and was assured that she was doing just fine. It is important to understand that settlement is more than just adding up the collections and sending out the checks. After you determine how much is collected, then you have to determine how much of the collected funds go to other places. For example, 'tax increment financing' where a portion of real estate can be set aside by a town council for development. Then, the property taxes collected on the *new* development goes to the TIF district to offset the cost to the town for any infrastructure that is required for the development; and the amount of taxes collected on the pre-development property is distributed to the original town or city. Then there are 'tax abatements.' Once an abatement is approved by the political sub-division, it has to be considered 'in settlement' and removed from the assessed value of the property abated. Also, there are many different kinds of deductions and exemptions on property taxes allowed by the state: homestead deductions, veteran's deductions, mortgage deductions, etc. These deductions also come off of the assessed valuation of the property, lowering the amount to be taxed. There are many, many of these deductions and exemptions, and all have to be calculated into the total assessment before any of the funds are disbursed. This vast amount of information goes on a huge form that the deputy sends to the State Auditor's office. The state settlements deputy approves it or calls us with questions. And so, eventually the first settlement deputy retired and moved on and the new settlement deputy continued to work really hard to master the job and meet the deadline. Well, she met the deadline and it was approved by the state, so she sent the checks to the appropriate sub-divisions.

Imagine my surprise when I picked up the local paper one evening after work and read that the local school superintendent said they would not have enough money for their budgets and it was the auditor's fault. Wait, what??? Now, I had known this man for a very long time, and he never even gave me the courtesy of a head's up phone call. I had no idea what he was talking about.

Needless to say, when I went to work the next morning I immediately sat down with my settlement deputy to try and figure out what had happened. Apparently she had miscalculated some deductions and assessments for the school and that meant their collections were down. I called the superintendent and asked him to please come in and see me and let me know what I could do to help. Come to find out, he had come to the office and looked at the settlement figures, but never bothered to say anything to me personally. It turned out there was another school corporation in the same situation, but their superintendent was kind enough to call me and let me know how to 'fix it' for him. They both just needed a letter from me explaining what had happened and how it would be corrected. Problem solved.

I did have a local reporter come to my office and do a story on the settlement problems. He was from my hometown, twenty-five miles down the road, and I knew him and his family very well. He listened carefully while I explained what happened and told him that it really was just an error by a new employee learning the job. However, I was responsible for what happened in the auditor's office so I would take the blame. At no time did I mention her name or let her be humiliated, that is not how I fly. My office, my responsibility.

I talked with my settlement deputy for a long time and she finally decided she really didn't want that job, it was too stressful. In the meantime, one of my former deputy clerks was having trouble with my successor in the clerk's office, so I asked her if she would like to move to the auditor's office and be my settlement deputy. I really thought she would do a great job. She agreed, and I was right. She spent a lot of time learning; many phone calls to the state settlement deputy (he was a wonderful man to work with); and really mastered that job. In fact, after she became very comfortable with it, she realized that the original settlement deputy (the one who retired) had often made mistakes. But instead of correcting them, she had adjusted (cooked) the books and then told people the taxes just weren't paid, so they couldn't be distributed. I was furious, but she was long gone. I always felt like that was the reason she left; she knew I would eventually figure it out, because I am a hands-on officeholder. Glad she was gone.

After the settlement calculations are completed, and it has been sent to the state, then we need to put those funds into our books so that we can distribute them. I got so tickled because this was one of the most difficult things for my settlement deputy to understand. I am a huge believer that it is so much harder to learn something if you don't understand why you need to do it and how it fits into the entire picture. 'Fund accounting' is something I learned as auditor (and I am very good at it), but for some reason it took my exceptionally bright deputy a while to understand it. I kept trying to explain the whole picture, but she was just stuck on this part...

The auditor collects all of the money (except taxes) for the county, so that it can be distributed to all of the other sub-divisions, but we don't put the money in the bank, the county treasurer does that. Every time someone brought us money, usually at the end of the month, we gave them a quietus (Latin for receipt) and took the money to the treasurer's office. Then the treasurer deposited it into the bank. However, for us to disburse that money, we had to get it receipted into 'our books.' When I took office I had one hundred and eight 'funds.' When I left office I believe the number of funds was around one hundred and thirty. Not all of the funds had to do with settlement. For example, payroll funds didn't go through settlement. But anything that was being sent to the other political sub-divisions did. County money just went into county funds. It was still in the bank, but in our books it was allocated according to separate funds. Every time the auditor wrote a check, it had to show on the check which fund it was coming from. The treasurer took care to balance the bank, the Auditor took care to balance the county books. The first two or three times my deputy did settlement I had to sit beside her and explain about the funding, and it sure was fun when the light bulb came on and she 'got it.' From that point on I never, ever worried about settlement being done correctly. Never ever.

Settlement deadline was December 31, but that was not our only hard financial deadline. By January 31 of each year, a complete financial report of all of those one hundred and thirty funds had to be published and sent to the state. Now, that was not the only deadline for January 31. Employees would start asking for their W-2 forms by about January 5, and we would tell them, "You will have it by January 31, that is the law." That was the federal deadline, and although it never took us that long, we still couldn't have them done in just a week.

I personally did the financial report, and I will say that is definitely how I learned about county finances. The year before I became Auditor, Mary B had suggested that I study her previous financial report so she would be there to answer questions. I took her report and all of the ledgers from the previous year over to the clerk's office and put them in the back conference room. Fortunately it was not a big election year, so I had a bit more time. When I could, I would go back there and research. I would look at the financial form, then go through the ledgers and find the matching number. I had a bit of an idea about county financing, (I was in my eighth year of office) but I was blown away by how much there was to learn. During my last year in office I suggested that my successor do the same thing; take the ledgers home and study. But he never did. Actually, when he took office, he gave that job to the settlement deputy. I'm not sure he ever really understood the county's finances. But I sure did. Good thing too, since being the fiscal/financial officer for the county was a large part of my job. Good thing to know.

State Board of Accounts—As Auditor

When I became auditor, a different person from the State Board of Accounts was handling state auditor meetings. He was very knowledgeable and incredibly funny. He started every meeting telling us jokes and sharing stories of his trials and tribulations as a father of two little boys. Two little very active boys. Two little, very energetic boys. Two little, extremely rambunctious little boys. We would be laughing until the tears ran. After all, almost all of us in the room were parents, some were grandparents, and we all had lots of stories of our own; however he told the best ones. But noth-

Pay The People... Bills... Political Sub Dvisions 199

ing topped the story of the wonderful, special anniversary weekend he spent with his wife, away from those happy little boys, only to find out a few months later, there might be another energetic little boy. He kept us on pins and needles until the big announcement— just a sweet little girl. Oh the relief. Then the stories started about how the sweet little girl ran the show and handled the two little boys. I never had an opportunity to meet his wife, but I sure wish I could have. Recently, all these years later, I read where one of those little boys grew up to be a State Board of Accounts Examiner. Imagine that. I bet he entertains the crowd as well as his dad did.

When the state meetings were located outside of Indianapolis, the SBA folks would often come to the hospitality room to socialize with everyone in the evening. It really gave us a nice opportunity to get to know them on a more personal level. It also made it easier, if you needed to call their office, to really know the person you were talking to.

The attendance at these meetings was usually 200-300 people, so it was impossible for them to take very many questions. As a result, they had a question box. They asked us to write down our questions and put them in the box, then that evening, after the meeting, they would look up the answers and go through them with us the next day. That was very helpful, but once in a while there would be a question (of course no names were attached) that had absolutely nothing to do with county government. For example, one time someone put in a question asking about a novelty item passed out by one of our vendors and what was it for. He didn't have a clue, but he was good sport and tackled those questions too.

The SBA examiners who conducted the state meetings were not the same people who came out to the counties to examine the books. These were field examiners, and the same people didn't come every year. It wasn't uncommon to start over with a new group every year. We never knew when they were coming, they just showed up and asked for the books. They did every office individually, but they worked out of the auditor's office because that is where most of the finances occurred. It was sometimes a bit frustrating because they didn't just check our books, they also checked procedures. There is often more than one way to interpret a rule or a procedure, and if they didn't like the way you did it, they would 'write you up'. Sometimes I think they just felt like they had to come up with something because nobody is perfect. Sometimes it made me mad, but sometimes I didn't care because my way was better.

Most of the time when they came, they helped us work through any problems. They answered questions, made suggestions, and just generally guided us. After they completed the audit, they would write up a report on each office, and the county in general, then present it to the commissioners. Each officeholder was required to be present in case the commissioners had any questions or concerns about the report. There were two times I was written up—once as clerk because they didn't like the way we paid our jurors. Well, one of my judges went nuts when I brought that to his attention and he told me he was not changing. I reminded him that it was SBA that wanted the change, not me, so he wrote a letter to them stating that he liked our procedures and he was not changing, and therefore I would not be able to comply. His letter became part of the final report and that was that. When I was auditor, I was required to maintain an inventory of the county's assets. From highway equipment, to computers, adding machines, desks, etc. There was a state form that each officeholder was to fill out when they got rid of something or bought something. Of course, nobody could remember to use it, me included, so I was always behind on that. Eventually I started putting all of that information on a spread sheet and asked the different offices to just fill out the change sheet, once a year. Well, the SBA wanted me to continue using the state form, but I told them I thought the spread sheet was better, more accurate, and easier for everyone to understand. They agreed, but wrote me up anyway. I think at least five times. Whatever.

Probably one of my biggest frustrations was when they were working with my financial report. Every year in January, it is the responsibility of the auditor to compile a complete annual financial report of the county and send it to the state. It needed to be published before it could be sent, so even though the official deadline was January 31, I had to have it completed in time to meet the newspaper printing deadline. The financial report had to be published before it was sent to state, and a copy of the legal ad proving that it had been published had to be sent with the report.. So the actual deadline to have it completed was long before January 31. I was really glad I had taken the time during my holdover year to study all of that when it came time to do my first report. I found it made the job a great deal easier, and it was ironic, the report was based on Mary B's last year in office.

Pulling together this report is something that I always did myself; I never delegated it to a deputy. They were all so busy in January with the end of one year and obligations for the new year, that I just did it. It takes a long time to pull the figures. Even though we sort of had a computer printout, it didn't encompass the entire financial situation, so I had to do a certain amount of digging for numbers right out of the ledger books. When I left office, all one hundred and thirty funds had to be accounted for. Plus, it had to balance to the penny.

I really worked hard on this report, and, because I often was interrupted, or had to spend a day in a meeting, I stayed later and sometimes even took it home with me. I always used the ML King holiday to work on this report, either at home or in the office, with nobody else there. Sometimes if I got stuck and simply couldn't find an error that was keeping me from balancing, I would ask my settlement deputy to run some totals for me. She was a whiz on a calculator and she usually found the mistake.

Once this report was balanced, I sent it off to the paper for the legal ad. Then I ran copies for all three commissioners and all seven county council members. Some of them really appreciated the information and some of them didn't even read it. But they could never say they weren't given the financial information of the county. Then I would put it away and not give it another thought until the state board of accounts field examiners showed up.

The financial report was their guideline for auditing my books. And it never failed—no matter how hard I worked or how certain I was that the financial form was balanced, they found errors. I came to realize that it wasn't so much math errors as it was the examiners handling the funds at the state a bit differently than we handled them at the county level. There was never any money missing, it was just a matter of us putting money in one place and them preferring it to be in a different place. The bottom line was always the same, but brother, that was frustrating to me. I would adjust our record keeping to be in compliance and then it would happen all over again the next year when a different set of examiners came in.

However, overall I always felt that the SBA was a good thing for all of the political sub-divisions in the state. Not only as an auditing mechanism to help keep the citizens informed about all levels of their government, but also as helpers and teachers for the very difficult job of local government. Not all local officials shared my opinion—some didn't like them at all—but I always had a much more positive opinion of the SBA than a negative opinion. And most of the people I knew and worked with from that agency were just outstanding folks.

Since I left county government, I have lived in two other states. I know that is not like some folks who have lived all over the place, but the one thing I noticed is that the local governments didn't seem to have the same support from state agencies that we had. I know there are some who would say, "Why do you want those people looking over your shoulder, telling you what to do, and auditing your books?" But I found it comforting to have a variety of departments, with people I could trust, to call on for help. Local government is complicated, and we didn't have professionally trained county managers. We all depended on those folks and even though, as in all cases, I liked and got along better with some than others, I found all of them to be sincere in their desire to help us be better elected officials. Who can argue with that?

Deputy Auditors

I only had a staff of seven full-time deputies in the auditor's office, making it much easier to manage, but each of those deputies really had big jobs. One thing about the auditor's office—we were the 'conduit' for the county. Since there was no county manager, the auditor's office was thrown into that role by default. We paid all of the county's bills, paid all of the county's people, and put together the county's budget so individual department budgets were submitted to the auditor. That meant the staff was sometimes put in the position of having to tell department heads things that they didn't always want to hear. The very term 'auditor' means I'm going to check your work, and if you don't get it right you will have to fix it; and folks don't always want to hear that. I tried to have my deputies' backs as much as I could, and when someone was flagrant, then I stepped in and took over the situation, but most of the time each deputy settled her own problems.

Checks sent from the auditor's office required two signatures; the auditor and the county treasurer. Generally the treasurer actually signed her name, and they used a signature stamp for mine, one original was all that was required, so the deputy auditors had it a bit easier.

There was not as much 'crossover' work between deputy auditors as there was with deputy clerks. We didn't have as much of the general public coming in and out of the office. We dealt more with real estate and title people, and of course anyone wanting access to the commissioners or county council members, plus other department heads and county employees. Each gal pretty much became the expert in her job and didn't get too involved in other areas of the office.

I brought three of my deputy clerks with me to the auditor's office, again because of the political change that was necessary. And of course, I later added another deputy clerk after all the chaos of her suspension and firing by the new clerk. The three remaining deputy auditors had each been there for many years and worked for the two auditors who preceded me. They welcomed the new gals in with kindness and grace and it wasn't long until we had a pretty cohesive staff—or so I thought.

One of the things I learned as clerk, from an auditor with the State Board of Accounts, was to be very cautious of any employee who says she can never be gone for any length of time because nobody else can do their job. The auditor said that is a red flag, and often means they have something to hide. I had never thought of that before, but I did remember hearing the payroll deputy in the auditor's office make that comment. So, when I took over I immediately had her start training my first deputy for payroll. That is one job that must get done every two weeks, no matter what. People get so testy when they don't get paid or if their checks are late. Go figure. Well, it turns out that this particular lady had an enormous amount of freedom to do her job, because the previous auditor was not as detail oriented as I am. She was not prepared for me to come in and start working with everyone closely enough to learn a lot about their jobs. Remember, I had been stung by my child support deputy in the clerk's office, and I was not going to let that happen again. Part way through my first year as auditor we purchased some new payroll and financial software. We had been using the original custom programs and they were woefully outdated. Of course, I was interested in the technology so I spent as much time learning the software as my staff did. The payroll deputy did not care for my involvement, so, she decided to retire. Okay, remember, nobody is irreplaceable. I had learned that lesson well as clerk, so I asked my first deputy to take over payroll full-time, along with the HR duties that came with it. We decided she would just learn the new program, and we would discontinue the old program when the original payroll deputy left, then she didn't have to mess with the new software.

My property records deputy worked part-time for Mary B. I offered her the full-time position when the full-time person that was there left because that gal was a Democrat and didn't like me. That was okay, because I didn't much care for her either, and eventually learned that she made an incredible mess of the department. Fortunately, the one who stayed to work for me was wonderful at the job, cleaned up the mess, added the geographical information systems (GIS) work to her already full load, then after I left, she went on to run for office and win. I'm sure the current auditor misses her. She was an incredibly hard worker, in fact, her husband owned a restaurant in downtown Plymouth and she used to go there on her lunch hour and help wait tables then come back to work in my office. We should all have such a wonderful work ethic.

There were too many people who worked for me over the years to name individually. Some were there when I started, some came and went—often to other positions in the county. They were all great and I'm glad I had the opportunity to work with them and get to know them.

However, two of the many ladies on my staff were with me the entire time that I served in office and three deputies went on to run for public office and serve as county officials. I like to think that working for me gave them the interest and confidence they needed to run for office. They were all wonderful deputies and I have no doubt every bit as good and capable as elected county officials.

Sharon Satorius started as my part-time election deputy when I took office in 1984. She served in that capacity until I needed a full-time traffic court deputy. She served as Traffic Deputy until I moved to the auditor's office and she became my First Deputy and her duties were payroll and HR. She remained in the auditor's office after my retirement for a few more years until she retired.

Neysa McFarland started in the Clerk's office during my second year in office as a general deputy. Eventually she helped Sharon with traffic court duties on a part time basis, and by the time we moved into the new facility, because of the growth in traffic court, she had become a full-time traffic deputy. When she joined me in the Auditor's office she became my Settlement Deputy. She continued to work in the Auditor's office until her retirement.

Mary Ann Miller started as my first full-time election deputy, then when we moved to the new office building she became my Small Claims Deputy in the clerk's office. She moved with me to the auditors office as a general deputy until she ran for clerk in 1996 and won. She served one term as clerk.

Karen Delp, my Judgment Deputy in the clerk's office came with me to the auditor's office and worked as a real estate deputy. She ran for County Treasurer in 1994 and won. She also served one term.

Janet Howard was a part-time property records deputy for Mary B and I asked her to stay and work full-time in the same job. She continued in that position until she ran for County Recorder in 2018 and won.

Sharon died in April, 2015 from pancreatic cancer. Neysa retired and lives in Colorado Springs, CO with her wife, Lizzie. Mary Ann and Karen are both now widowed and still living in Plymouth. Janet is still serving her first term as Recorder.

In my eight years as auditor, I never really had much trouble with deputies. Of course there was turnover, one retired, another one had to quit because she was beginning to have some memory issues, one moved out of state, and of course the two who became elected officials. As I had mentioned earlier, I always thought it was important that you be loyal to your staff and let them know you 'had their back.' In the case of my deputy auditors, I always felt comfortable that, with one exception, they had my back too.

At the end of my second term as auditor, just as I was planning my exit from county government and the move to another stage of my life, my husband had a heart attack and stroke. This was during my last month in office. Needless to say, I was a bit distracted in regards to what was happening at work, so I was quite saddened when I found out later that one of my deputies was quite upset with me during that time. Apparently she had asked me for some help in a particular area and I did not respond the way she wanted me to. I have no recollection of that conversation, but I was told she was quite angry and vocal about my telling her no. Earlier that year she had been dealing with some heavy duty personal issues with her sister, so I tried to cut her as much slack as I could regarding her attendance and some work issues. Guess she didn't feel that I was entitled to the same courtesy when my husband was sick. Maybe she didn't realize that bosses are people, too.

With a few exceptions I had very good experiences with most of the ladies who worked in the clerk's office and auditor's office while I was their boss. I hold them in the highest regard and know that I could never have done it without them.

My campaign 'portrait' when I ran for Auditor in 1990.

The 1990 County brochure—kind of looks like a 'Zoom' meeting of today.

Being sworn in as Auditor by Superior Court No. 2 Judge Dean Colvin. I don't remember what we were laughing about, but we always had a good time working together.

Combined Christmas dinner with the deputies from the Auditor's office and the Treasurer's office, along with me and the deputies who were moving with me to the auditor's office. Mary B took the picture.

Me with my first set of County Commissioners, Ray Borrgren, Clark Dare, and Glenn Overmyer.

Mary B and I at the ground breaking ceremony for the Oakhill Avenue project. I convinced her to come since she was in town and worked on the project a lot longer than I did.

A County Council budget hearing.

Me in my office in the County Building, the one furnished by items I found around the building that nobody was using.

Me in the auditor's outer office, 'helping out.'

My auditor's staff in the last part of my first term.

Our final Auditor's Christmas party at my house. Tom was in the hospital so it was pretty low key. Sharon took the picture.

Part 4 - Other Stuff That Mattered

"Cultivate a network of trusted mentors and colleagues. Other people can give us the best insight into ourselves—and our own limitations. We must have the courage to ask for help and to request feedback to expand our vision of what's possible."

—Maria Castañón Moat

Chapter 16
Meetings, Meetings, and More Meetings.

Four-hundred-and-ninety-four sets of minutes. That is approximately how many times I took and typed up minutes during my sixteen years in office. Four-hundred-and-ninety-four times. I vowed I would never take another set of minutes in my life. But it never failed, after I left office, every organization I belonged to always asked me to be secretary and take the minutes. Of course they did, I was good at it. I had four-hundred-and-ninety-four opportunities to practice. And council and commissioner minutes are very detailed and involved, and must be correct—they are public record. Four-hundred-and-ninety-four sets of minutes.

Not all of those minutes were for council or commissioners because you see, along with all of the other duties required by the clerk or the auditor, there are boards and committees that you must serve on. Some are statutory, like the County Election Board, or the Old Records Commission, and some are by commissioner appointment, like the Job Classification Committee. And some are because your fellow officeholders and department heads beg and plead and bargain to get you to serve, like the Technical Committee—and then they beg and plead and bargain for you to take the minutes because you are 'so good at it.' Of course I am, I have done it four-hundred-and-ninety-four damn times.

Statutory Boards

The County Election Board, the Board of Review, and the Old Records Commission are three of the statutory boards that I served on. The Election Board as clerk, the Board of Review as auditor, and the Old Records Commission as clerk and auditor. No doubt, the County Election Board took the most work. Indiana code 3-6-5-8 is the law that stated the clerk would be secretary. Now, I had always been under the delusion that 'secretary' meant take, prepare, and disburse minutes of the meeting. But since I was the only full-time member of this board, I called the meetings, did all of the meeting prep, ran the meetings (even though we did have a president), and did all of the followup of the meetings. I guess you could call that 'extended secretary duties.' I told the other election board members when to be there, what we needed to discuss, and pretty much how it should be taken care of (since I was the only one who knew how to look up the laws), although we did take votes on any issues of importance. I don't remember ever not having a 3-0 decision, but if we did, it must have not been very important.

Election board duties varied depending on if it was an election year and the type of election we were conducting. It is interesting that, on every election day, all three of us wore many hats. On election day, the other board members were voting machine mechanics, and their job was to be available to trouble shoot and help with any machine problems or questions. My job was primarily dealing with voter registration issues.

Later, we all three reverted to election board members and certified any absentee ballots that came in that day's mail. Then the other two members delivered those last minute absentee ballots to the appropriate precinct. We also acted as election board members if there was any type of question that required we all act on it and vote, which was very rare during my tenure. After the polls closed and the results started coming in, we became the canvassing board. They recorded the votes on the big canvassing sheets while I took care of the precinct workers who were bringing in the tallies and their supplies. After all of the precincts reported in, I joined them as a canvassing board member and we certified the results; unless for some reason we needed to wait until the next day.

There is no doubt, that in Marshall County, and all over the state, the election board members were very dependent on the clerk. Except in the very largest counties, we basically ran the show, and the part-time election board members were just not as knowledgeable of the whole process. That is okay, I liked bossing them around.

Fortunately the Old Records Commission didn't meet very often. Only when there were specific requests made to destroy records. The commission was made up of: the circuit court judge; the clerk; auditor; recorder; president of the board of county commissioners; superintendent of the school located in the county seat (Plymouth); and the clerk-treasurer of the county seat. Indiana Code 5-15-6-1(c) is the law that stated the clerk would be secretary.

This group only met when there were requests for destruction of records by any of the political sub-divisions in the county, or public entities. This was the time that many courthouses, city halls, schools, libraries, and other entities were struggling with space issues. Remember, we were just getting into digital record keeping—it was still very new then—so all these people were dealing with mounds of records stuffed into overflowing filing cabinets, many of them down in basements and cellars of very old buildings. Nobody ever wanted to go into those areas and deal with the spiders and cobwebs, so the records just stayed there taking up space.

Initially there wasn't a lot of guidance from the state regarding old records. We pretty much knew personnel records and financial records should be kept. And of course anything of historical value should be kept, including the big, leather-bound ledger books that courthouses had used for years. Then the state decided to put together an official retention guide for the destruction of public records. It was developed by the staff of the Indiana State Archives, and signed into law in 1991. It was incredibly helpful and made our job much easier.

Over the years, the State Archivist attended many of the clerk's meetings to guide us on how to handle record retention, as well as the historical records we all had. As it became more evident that counties needed to clear some space, he developed record retention rules for micro-filming the records before they were destroyed (the ones that the law said must be kept). Marshall County already had some records on microfilm, but not all that many. I thought it was a great idea to start clearing out the records, so I went to the council and commissioners for permission and funding to hire some part-time people to do that job. While I was working with my county officials, I also worked with the state staff to develop a 'how to' manual to be used during this process. The commissioners approved, and eventually the council agreed to fund it, so we moved many of the filing cabinets that housed these records into the vacant third floor room in the county building, hired two ladies to do the filming, and got after it. When we moved into the new courts building I moved the filming into the basement of the courts building so all of my people were in the same building.

I know the filming went on throughout my tenure as auditor, but I have no idea if they are still putting records on microfilm; if they have switched to digitizing the records; or if they stopped altogether. I do hope they kept that department funded; it was a very important part of maintaining Marshall County's history.

The Board of Review was an interesting group—now called the Property Tax Assessment Board of Appeals, or 'PTABOA'. Entities that were receiving a property tax exemption—churches, fraternal organizations, other charitable organizations—were required to file a state form that nothing had changed, or if there were changes, to list them. Then the board would meet and go over the forms and determine if anyone needed to have the exemption removed. For example: a church might own a house they had used as a parsonage, so it would be exempt from property taxes along with other church property. Then the pastor might decide to purchase a home, so the church rents the parsonage, therefore the parsonage would no longer be exempt from property taxes, but the other church property would remain exempt. Basically, it amounted to, "was there a change in use of the property, and if so, did it generate income?" We didn't have a lot of changes from year to year, but there were always a few.

The Board was made up of the auditor, assessor, and treasurer, as well as two citizens, one Democrat and one Republican, appointed by the county commissioners. The meetings usually lasted about one or two days. The auditor was the secretary, but we only met once or twice a year. They were good guys to work with, and even though both parties were represented, there was nothing political about the work we did, so everyone got along very well. One thing of importance; the Democrat member of the board introduced me to Werther's caramel candy. He always had some in his pocket for all of us, and I'm very glad he did—I really like Werthers.

Commissioner Appointed Committees

The Job Classification Committee is the one that I most remember, having served as a member in both my capacity as the clerk and as the auditor. When I took office as clerk, there were very few, if any, real job descriptions in the county. What they did have was woefully inadequate; often a salary was determined by what door the employee walked in, or who they worked for. It had just evolved over the years and really wasn't fair. Many of the employees were beginning to grumble about the lack of consistency in pay, so they were talking about starting a union. Public employment unions were not common in Indiana at that time, but they were beginning to become more vocal and encouraging public employees to speak out about forming a union. Now, I knew that would never go over in Marshall County, however I did feel like some of the employees had a case.

I asked Mary B if she might consider working with me to get the commissioners to consider looking into job classification as a way to make the job descriptions current, and maybe even out the salaries a bit. She thought it was a good idea, and since she was auditor at the time, she 'worked on' the commissioners until they agreed to hear a proposal. We invited one of the county vendors to a commissioners' meeting and they explained to the board what job classification was all about, how it worked, and how it was maintained once a classification had been adopted. The board agreed and sent out proposals for bids. They picked a company and the work began.

The first item was to appoint a job classification committee to work with the consultant to develop the classification and to oversee the maintenance of the classification. The consultant suggested they appoint one commissioner, one council person, someone to represent the appointed department heads, and someone to represent the other elected officials. The auditor was an automatic member of the committee because all of the information would need to flow through the auditor's payroll desk. Well, guess who was appointed to represent the elected officials. I didn't really mind, I wanted to learn all about the job classification anyway.

One of the first things we did was have a meeting with the employees, the committee, and the consultant. He gave them a brief outline of what this was all about, and what would be expected of them. Then, each employee was given an opportunity to write a job description of their job since they knew best what they did every day. The consultant had forms for everyone to use, so there would be some consistency. It took a while to get all of them motivated to get the job done, but eventually they were all turned in and the real work began.

The committee met with the consultant and learned how to 'grade' different types of job descriptions. This gave him a guideline as to how to grade the descriptions turned in from Marshall County. We practiced on examples, not the real thing. After a few months, he returned to the county with all the various jobs classified and it was up to the commissioners and council to determine how they wanted to pay. Now, there are a lot of variables that go into determining the salary, but personal identity was not supposed to be one of those variables. Believe me, in a county our size, when many of the people had worked there for years and years, that is a very difficult variable to ignore. But we did our best.

Of course, adjustments were going to have to be made, some folks were underpaid for their classification and some were overpaid. The consultant recommended that we increase the underpaid salaries, but leave the overpaid salaries alone. He didn't think it would be very popular for the board and council to start taking money away from employees. I heartily agreed. By the time it was all said and done, I think most of the employees were happy, some of course, not so much. But the pay scale in Marshall County was certainly more balanced than it had been before.

One of the most difficult areas of job classifications was maintaining them as the various job responsibilities and duties changed throughout the county. Sometimes those changed because a new person was in charge of a department, or sometimes they changed because statutes added responsibilities to a job. When that occurred, there was a form the consultant gave us to update the job description. That was filed in the auditor's office, and then the auditor made a record of it and sent it on to the consultant. After they had 're-classified' the job, (or not, if reclassification wasn't needed), they would return it to the auditor with any recommendations. The auditor would present it to the committee for approval. If something required a change in salary, then it would have to go to the council. Some of the department heads or elected officials would complain that it was not fair—maybe the new officeholder was an especially good writer, so they could 'build up' a job description, but the consultant could see right through that so it wasn't a factor. The job classification firm worked all over the state, for both counties and municipalities. They had a great deal of knowledge as to what work was done in each department. It was pretty tough to fool them.

A couple of years after I moved over to the auditor's office, I decided that some of the job descriptions in my office should be revised to reflect the changes I had made, and the state had made. Everything went fine, I sent them to the consultant, they looked them over and made recommendations and sent them back to me, then I presented the recommendations to the committee. The only problem came with the job description for the payroll/HR deputy. She was underpaid by about ten thousand dollars. Now, I'm smart enough to know, and I informed her, that nobody was going to get a ten thousand dollar wage increase in Marshall County. However, I told her I would present it to the committee and see if we could work out a compromise. She was fine with that.

Unfortunately some of the members of the committee were not even reasonable when they saw that discrepancy. Plus they made it personal. You can never make this stuff personal, it has to be based on the job responsibilities, not the person. The reason the consultant had increased the classification so much, was because by this time, as opposed to years earlier, people were beginning to sue public entities over payroll matters, and that made the job much more difficult. The thinking was, you have to pay enough for that position to entice the right person to take the job. If you didn't have the right person, too many mistakes could be made and that could cost the county a lot of extra money, in lawsuits, legal fees, and settlements.

But that did not matter to some of these members. Not only did they refuse to compromise, they wouldn't consider any salary increase. Well, that made me mad. Not so much because it was my deputy, but more because it totally undermined the job classification in general. I had spent hours, and hours, and hours, as clerk and auditor, on the job classification: making sure it was done right; helping other department heads understand it; working with the consultant to answer questions and concerns; basically doing anything anybody needed, because I so firmly believed the salaries should be based on the job, not the person, or where they worked. I was really, really angry. So I quit the committee. Auditor is a tough enough job, why add all the extra duties of administering the job classification if the committee wasn't going to follow it. Might as well throw the money we paid for the classification, and the maintenance fees, up in the air and set it on fire, at least then it would generate some heat instead of it being totally wasted.

I turned in my letter of resignation to the commissioners and they were not happy. Nobody in the county had as much job-classification experience as I did, since I had been involved from the very beginning. The next thing I know, a day or two later, there is a letter to the editor from the best friend of one of our commissioners, who hated me because I had to fire his wife back when I was clerk. It was a scathing misrepresentation of what I had wanted from the job classification for my payroll deputy. First of all, the letter writer had no idea how any of this worked, so he just wrote what his commissioner buddy told him to write, and a great deal of it was incomplete and misleading. I know they thought I would take a hit from the letter. But they really underestimated me. I sat right down and wrote an extensive rebuttal. And since I knew how it all worked (way better than either of them) I really let them have it, and included my comments about wasting all that taxpayer money if we didn't use the classification. Not to mention, I'm a better writer and my letter made way more sense. I figured that was that, and I would now have more time to concentrate on other auditor duties. I did agree to train whomever they chose to administer job classification and take my place on the committee.

Next thing I know, the other two commissioners came into my office and asked me to please reconsider. They agreed with the comments in my letter; said that the first one should never have been written against me; and that they would assure that the committee worked with me to come up with a compromise for that deputy's salary. I agreed to continue as administrator, because I really did like doing it. But I just didn't understand why they always had to make it so hard.

When Marshall County first began to automate and use computers in the late seventies and early eighties, there were no pre-written software programs. The county worked with a firm from South Bend and all of the software was custom written. The fellow that worked with the county to get this done was a real sweetheart and came to know all of us very well. He lived in Marshall County and really enjoyed working with us. Eventually he left the software company and started his own business as a consultant. The county hired him on a part-time basis and it really worked well for a long time. However, he was working out of the county building and there came a time when he was putting in enough hours that the commissioners felt they may need to make him a full-time employee in order to comply with federal employment laws. He did not want to be full time, so they decided to search for someone to head up the 'computer department', as they called this one man office. They formed a committee of some of the more knowledgeable office holders (not me) to advertise and see if we could find someone to take the job. Eventually a young man did apply, he wanted to move back to Indiana, his family was here, and he had a degree in computer technology or whatever they called it then. He was the best choice, and they hired him for the job. To my knowledge, he is still with the county.

Of course, not long after he started, he realized that the auditor was the hub of the county, so he and I got to be good friends. Some of the other department heads felt like the time was right to form a Technology Committee to back up our IT director (formerly known as the computer guy), to oversee the acquisition of the equipment, the expansion of computer applications, etc. One of the main people involved in this was the Purdue Extension Agent. He was not an employee of the county, he was paid by Purdue University, but he did oversee a large department and was pretty savvy in computer knowledge. He was made chairman of the committee, and it included the IT director, one commissioner, one council person, and one elected official. I was not involved. And then I was. Three of them came to me and asked me to be on the committee—remember the first paragraph of this chapter? I said no, I don't have time and I don't know enough about it. But they wanted me because I understood the financing and they would definitely need financing. So alright, I caved. And I must say it was an education. When the committee chairman and I went to the commissioners to get their 'blessing' to allow each office to have email (it was not a given back then) one of the commissioners said he didn't think that was necessary and, I quote, "That internet stuff is just a passing fad, I don't think we should spend any money on it." Well, I looked at the chairman, and he looked at me, and we each said, "We're done here, we won't take up any more of your time." Passing fad, my ass. Fortunately, the county did not stop there and they moved right on into the twenty-first century like everybody else, but it was touch and go there for a while.

I think where I was most valuable to this committee was helping them secure funds, through the budget, for updated computer equipment. We were meeting to discuss what would be needed to go into the budget request, when the council member on the committee asked if this would just be, "a one time purchase." I said, "No, computers are an ongoing thing and the county will be buying computer equipment, probably forever. It will always need to be replaced, or upgraded, or purchased because of our growth." Computer equipment as a "one time purchase"—really!? Even I knew that eventually there would be computers on every desk, both at work and at home, in every school, business, store—you name it—all over the world. How could anyone not living under a rock fail to understand that? I knew that. I was not a techie person at all, but I knew that. Computers were the way of the future. Good grief, didn't these people ever watch an episode of *The Jetsons*?

There were more committees I served on through the years, but I don't remember them all, or they were temporary. Besides, I didn't have time for any more committees. I already had to take more than four-hundred-and-ninety-four sets of minutes. That is enough for anyone in a lifetime, and I did it in sixteen years. Four-hundred-and-ninety-four sets of minutes. Notes taken, typed up, approved, filed, and occasionally referred to. Four-hundred and ninety-four damn times.

Chapter 17
On the Record, Off the Record—
Be Very Careful

Everyday now, I hear something on TV, or social media, or read in the papers, that 'the press is the enemy of the people.' NO THEY ARE NOT. I am a true believer in the freedom of the press, even though they weren't always kind to me as an elected official. I agree with our founding fathers—freedom of the press is so important that it is listed in the very first amendment to the constitution.

Gov. Frank O'Bannon created a position called the Public Access Counselor in 1998 by Executive Order. This office provides advice and assistance concerning Indiana's public access laws to members of the public and government officials and employees (specifically the Access to Public Records Act and the Open Door Law). The Indiana General Assembly then made the office permanent by statute in 1999. The Access to Public Records and Open Door Laws are also sometimes called "The Sunshine Laws."

Since my very first day in office, I have tried to serve with as much transparency (before 'transparency' became a buzz word) as I could. Except for the few exceptions as outlined in the statutes, I never kept anyone from getting legal information from my office. However, I didn't think it was necessary for me to be the town crier, so I tried to be careful in what I 'put out there' for the press.

I was lucky. I had two local newspapers, *The Plymouth Pilot* and the local section of *The South Bend Tribune*. This section of the Tribune covered not only Marshall County, also Fulton County, Starke County, Kosciusko County, and La Porte County, all in north central Indiana. Both papers had reporters who I came to know and respect, and I think they felt the same way about me. But they were still the press, and not everything was on the record. And I learned that the hard way.

Early in my second year as clerk, one of the school corporations in my county was thinking about switching from an appointed school board to an elected school board. At that time there was a mix in the county; some corporations had elected boards, some were appointed by various officials. Of course it is always the citizens who decide it is time for an elected board, never a member of the current board or a school administrator. One day a resident of that school corporation came into the office and asked to talk to me. We were standing at the front counter and he asked me about what it would take to have an election to change over to an elected school board. Well, we weren't whispering, but it was a private conversation. I gave him the information he needed, told him to let me know if they wanted to proceed, and turned around to go back to my desk. The reporter from the Tribune was standing there and asked me if this school corporation was switching over. I answered that some of the citizens were interested and were in the process of getting preliminary information. He said okay and I never gave it another thought, until I picked up the next day's paper and saw a headline that this corporation was switching over to an elected school board. I about died. I had no idea if this was confidential information or not. I hadn't thought to ask, but I didn't think they wanted it in the paper yet. But there it was, and it was my fault. Nobody from that community ever said anything to me about the article, and we did go ahead and have a special election to change over the board, but lesson learned. Never again did I just 'answer' a reporter's questions without making sure whether we were on or off the record.

The local reporters spent a great deal of time in my office, because they covered all of the public meetings and of course, all aspects of the election. During the fiasco following the 1996 election and recount, they were in the courthouse almost daily. Fortunately, the reporters from the local papers stayed right on top of all of that, and one Pilot reporter even wrote a great article about how I, and the other five clerks in the district, had been shut out of decisions being made by the state regarding the congressional recount. He came in and interviewed me on the spot and it was nice to have my side of the story 'out there' for the public to read. Of course, by the time all that mess was over, I had not been treated well by the CBS affiliate TV station in South Bend, but it wasn't the station's fault. Their reporter simply wasn't interested in my side of the story, which I found to be incredibly unprofessional. After that 'investigation' was over, and everything was found to be in order, I was surprised, and pleased, that articles about it were published in different parts of the state. Many of my fellow clerk's sent me copies so I would know that everyone knew we had done it right. They knew the election was clean, of course, but they wanted me to know that the word was out around the state.

Everyone knows that when it comes time for an officeholder to be reelected, there is the advantage of the incumbency. Some of that comes from the general covering of local government, but it was not uncommon for the local reporters to also call me just to ask a question. They might have been working on a story about something that didn't necessarily involve me or my office, but needed information my office could provide. And they always asked to talk to me directly, and I complied unless I was not available. I have no doubt that a lot of my good coverage came because I was cooperative with them, and sometimes they even quoted me or gave me credit in those articles. Every little bit of publicity helps.

After I moved to the auditor's office, it was not as common to have the press cover me personally. Of course, they were in attendance at all of the meetings, and they often asked me questions about what was going on in the meetings. I tried really hard to get them an agenda ahead of time; that way if there was something they were not interested in on the agenda they could schedule their day around it. Also, I was really careful about notifying the press when we had special meetings. They always had a copy of the regular schedule, but if something came up and an extra meeting was required, I was really good about letting them know—even about the executive meetings that the press could not attend. They trusted that I would not let any county body meet privately for anything not listed in the statute, and they were right. If a group did meet without notifying the press, I considered it an illegal meeting and refused to attend.

In an earlier chapter, I spoke of the lawsuit the sheriff's deputies filed against the county. Well, before the suit was filed, one of the deputies wrote a scathing letter to the editor about the commissioners. Even though I was not mentioned, I felt like it was really unfair, especially because a great deal of it was inaccurate. So I convinced the commissioners to come in to the county building on a Saturday morning and work with me to write a rebuttal letter. They just shouldn't let something like that pass. They knew I was a good communicator so they agreed. However, this was a private meeting, and had nothing to do with county business as far as making decisions or doing anything official. While we were working on the letter, a reporter from the Tribune came in and wanted to know why we were meeting. Since I had not advertised the meeting she thought we might be violating the open door laws. I explained to her exactly what was going on, that it was not a meeting, just a 'rebuttal conference' and promised that nothing else was being discussed. Since I had always been so straight with the press, she believed me and went on her way. Credibility is a great thing, but one really has to work hard to earn it.

During my sixteen years as an elected official, I never lost sight of the fact that I worked for the public. I was paid by tax dollars, my staff was paid by tax dollars, and my offices were funded by tax dollars. Every dime that was spent for the operation and maintenance of both the clerk and auditor's offices was advertised in the local paper. There were no secrets. I just didn't believe it was fair to the hardworking citizens in my county to pay for the operation of the county and not be up front where those monies went. I know it cost the county a lot to advertise the claims in legal ads twice a month; and I know the paper counted on the regular revenue. I did think it was a bit unfair that only the county had to advertise every time we paid the bills, and the other sub-divisions in the county (towns, library, schools, did not). They only had to advertise their budgets. Many times legislation was proposed to change that requirement, but we always lost out to the Indiana Press Association which of course supported their member papers and didn't want them to lose that revenue. I never forgot the old adage—you can't fight someone who buys ink by the barrel and paper by the roll. That may not be so true today, but it sure was back then.

When I think of the digital society we have become, I am glad that I don't have to deal with the misinformation that is often published on social media. My local papers worked very hard to make sure what they printed was accurate, and both papers published corrections if necessary. They sometimes even wrote an entire article if the error was big enough. I'm truly sad to see the print media industry shrinking. I can't say enough about how much it matters to a community to have a thriving local paper, to cover not only local sports, people, clubs, and other issues; but to be the watchdog they need to be for local government. Of course, it is up to each individual citizen to stay informed and there is no better way to do that than a local newspaper. They need to buy the paper and read it, really read it, especially the local government coverage. Local government matters, but so do the Sunshine Laws that are designed to keep local governments transparent and honest.

Chapter 18
Meeting More People From Around the State

Indiana County Auditors' Association

The ICAA, or as we called it, the Auditor's Association, met twice a year in the spring and fall. Again, they were state meetings called by the State Board of Accounts, but we hosted them. Because of the many, many various responsibilities of the auditor, the meetings were necessary to keep us up to date on legislative changes, and state rules and regulations.

Many of the vendors who called on counties were in attendance at these meetings because they knew that 'auditors' have the ear of the commissioners, who do most of the purchasing for the county. Vendors often hosted hospitality rooms, or maybe a specific vendor would take officials from a customer county out to dinner. Whatever the case, I always enjoyed the time I spent in the rooms and or at those dinners, getting to know my fellow county auditors from around the state. We had lots of discussions on 'how to.' For example, 'how do you do this or that' giving each other lots of ideas and tips. Everyone needed more staff, but the counties didn't have the money for more personnel, so it became very important to run the offices as efficiently as possible. I shared a lot of my organizational ideas and communication skills with other officeholders and learned a lot from them in return.

I think there were about six of us who had been clerks, and who were elected auditors at the same time. By the time we finished our terms as auditors we had all become great friends; and not just us, but many of our deputies, also.

In October of my first year as auditor, I was planning to attend the fall meeting scheduled for later that month. As it turned out, my son, Steve, was in a very bad accident and was hospitalized, then laid up for three months. Well, there was no way I could be gone, so I sent my deputies without me. Since they had been going to other meetings with me through the years, they also knew many of the people, which made it so much easier for them to go and enjoy the meeting. When they explained why I wasn't there, I got lots of calls and cards wishing me, and Steve, well.

I was very lucky, during that time that I could come and go as I needed from work. When Steve was in the hospital in South Bend, I would often spend the day with him, then go to the office when I got home in the evening and catch up on the mail, paperwork, messages, etc. I would leave a list for my staff if I needed something to be done the next day. Eventually, Steve was transferred to an Indianapolis hospital, so one day I drove home to attend the state budget hearings, then went back that night. After he was released from the hospital and we brought him home, he was not able to go school for a while. Indiana law required that the school corporation provide home schooling for his main subjects so he would not fall behind. He loved it. (Home schooling was not done very much back then). Tom and I would alternate days as to who stayed home with him, because it was easier than coming and going to our respective offices for short periods of time. It worked out very well until Steve was able to return to school after Christmas break. He really liked that staying home, in the recliner with his broken leg elevated, in front of the TV, being waited on—yeah, what a life for a fourteen year old! That was the perfect life for him. It was Steve. What can I say.

That was the only time I missed an auditor's association meeting, and I had never missed a clerk's meeting, so my attendance record was pretty good. I will always think that the lessons, friends, and activities from those meetings made me a better officeholder.

Association of Indiana Counties

AIC is the umbrella group to all of the affiliate associations in the state. Each elected county office had an affiliate association and all were members of AIC except the Sheriff's Association. All of the others—assessor, auditor, clerk, commissioners, coroners, county council, recorders, surveyors, and treasurers—were members. The president of each of the affiliates automatically served on the AIC Board of Directors. County highway engineers or supervisors, and the counties' IT directors, were represented on the board in an advisory capacity but could not vote.

In addition to being a state association, AIC was divided into six districts. Marshall County is in the Northwest District, and while I was auditor I served as president. As president, I was automatically a member of the AIC Board, a job that I really, really liked.

I got off to a rocky start with the AIC when I was still clerk. One of the first meetings we attended was the Legislative Conference held in January. This gave us an opportunity to learn about proposed legislation and to meet and talk with our local legislators, who had been invited to join us for lunch. After the meeting, some of us were chatting and I realized that they, along with me, thought that the clerks' association was not very important to AIC; and that most of what they did centered around the commissioners. Well, we had an opportunity to casually visit with the executive director of AIC at that time, so I said something along the lines of, "Why don't you do more for clerks?" Well, he was taken aback, and he said he thought they treated everyone the same, but we assured him they didn't. It really wasn't long after that conversation that I felt the AIC started paying more attention to all of the affiliates. And of course, just like the State Election Board, the Executive Director of the AIC and I became fast friends. He has since moved on, but we are still friends.

When my clerk colleagues and I started working on single-fee legislation, the AIC was very helpful to us, and assigned a staff member to keep us up to date as to what was happening at the state house. Remember, we were all working clerks, and we couldn't be in Indy on a moments notice, especially me, who lived the furthest away.

While I was still clerk, the AIC instituted an awards program. They honored an office holder for each affiliate and awarded an Outstanding County award to five individual counties. The "Outstanding County Official" award was determined by each affiliate. They determined how they wanted to pick their outstanding officeholder. I was fortunate to receive that award, "Outstanding Clerk of the Court" in 1985. I had no idea that our president had even considered me so it was quite an honor and quite a surprise.

In order to be awarded as one of the five Outstanding Counties, a nomination had to be sent to AIC, The criteria was based on how the county solved specific problems. Also, since the AIC encouraged cooperation with municipalities in the county, it was important that the nomination illustrated that. I decided that Marshall County should received one of these awards. I asked Mary B if she would sign our nomination if I wrote it, so that there would be signatures from a Democrat and a Republican. She agreed, so I got to work. I told the commissioners I was doing it, but I don't think they thought we would win. These awards were presented at the AIC annual meeting in the fall, at the banquet held on the last night of the conference. The counties receiving an award were all seated together in front of the stage, by county. That is how we knew we won one of the awards. Generally, the Chairman of the Commissioners would go on stage to receive the award, but my commissioners said that: since I wrote it; submitted it; and they didn't have anything to do with it; I should go up and represent our county and receive the plaque. I thought that was pretty nice and generous of them. Eventually, we received highway signs to put at the county line (from AIC, donated by a road sign vendor) stating that Marshall County was an Association of Indiana Counties Outstanding County. To my knowledge, no one ever nominated us again. If so, it would have been long after I left, but I don't think so.

The AIC annual conference was one of my favorites because it gave me the opportunity to see friends from around the state who did not serve as clerks or auditors when I did. All the vendors came, since all the officeholders were there, and they set up in the largest room in the facility like a trade show. Then we walked all around to see them and their wares, pick up any little gifts that they had, and get our card stamped that proved we had visited their booth. Once we got our vendor card filled up, we were eligible for the door prizes that many of them gave away.

One year, after we began using job classification in the county, I was attending an AIC annual meeting, and taking my time wandering around the trade show, visiting with the vendors. I always made it a point to stop and see the vendors we used, so I went to see my friends at Waggoner, Irwin, and Scheele, our job classification consultants. Their office is located in Muncie, Indiana, which also happens to be the home of Jim Davis, creator of Garfield the Cat. In his booth, they had a gift basket full of goodies with a very cute stuffed Garfield sitting on top. I just loved it, so of course I signed up. However, I rarely win raffless and I figured it was in vain. Well lo and behold, I *did* win that one and was the happy recipient of the basket *and* the Garfield. After I finished walking around the room, I was standing outside of the display hall chatting with a group of friends, showing them my cool prize when someone walked by, grabbed Garfield right out of the basket, and kept on walking. We were all just stunned. Then I got mad. A bit later, Kent Irwin from the consulting company walked by and I told him what had happened. Kent was stunned also.

I was disappointed to lose my Garfield, but I still had a basket full of nice goodies to take home, so I went on my way and forgot about it. Not long after that, Kent showed up in my office—I was still Clerk then—and handed me a brand new Garfield, just like the one taken from my basket. I was thrilled to death and Garfield sat on the shelf in the clerk's office, the auditor's office, and my office at home for many, many years, until he just wore out. A great reminder of a wonderful company and wonderful people, especially Kent and his wife, Pam, who became personal friends of Tom and I—golf together and dinners together, with lots of wine and lots of laughter.

Also, since I was a board member (and had a ribbon on my name badge to prove it), I sometimes got extra special attention from the vendors. The AIC conference was a blast, and I don't think I ever missed one. Sometimes I still wish I could attend.

Northwest District Auditor's Association

The NW District Auditor's Association is made up of the sixteen counties in the northwest corner of the state. We met from time to time throughout the district and heard various speakers having to do with Auditor issues, especially from our part of the state. I served as district president for two years until I decided to run for president of the NW district of AIC. These are the auditors who were the most helpful to me because we met so often, along with deputy auditors, that we all got to know each other very, very well. I tried my best as president to be available to answer any questions that newly elected auditors might have—just like was done for me when I started—as well as steer them in the right direction if I didn't have the answer. At my last meeting as president in December, we met in Cass County (Logansport) and our hosts gave me all of the cute Christmas ornaments they had made for table decorations as my 'leaving office' gift. I just loved them and still hang a few on my Christmas tree.

Association of Indiana Counties (AIC) Northwest District

When I decided to run for president of the district, it was mostly because I was tired of the guy who was in that position. He had held it for a few years and was a very controversial officeholder. He was an auditor, and was always fighting with his council, or commissioners, or other officeholders. I knew this, because his county was covered in the South Bend Tribune, which was read by most of us in that part of the state. When he announced he was going to run yet again for president, I decided to step up and give it a try. Well, lo and behold, I won. And I found out later that I won rather handily. I guess the other officeholders in the district didn't much care for him either. Apparently, elections in that capacity are not very common. The AIC staff usually had to beg someone to serve as a District President, or the same ones serve over and over, so they were thrilled that there was a 'contest.' It certainly brought more people to the meeting.

AIC district meetings are for all of the county officials in that district. Those are the same counties that make up the NW District Auditor's Association. However, not all of the officeholders attend. It tends to be the auditor, clerk, commissioners, surveyor, and the treasurer. Sometimes the recorder would go, but not very often. The purpose of the meetings was to go over legislative activities that affected county government. The various counties in the district took turns hosting these meetings, which were always dinner meetings. Of course, there was a social hour before dinner, hosted and paid for by the vendors, which gave everyone plenty of time to catch up with each other.

Generally, when attending these meeting, co-workers would ride together, especially if a commissioner went, because we could then use a county car. That gave us a good opportunity to visit and talk about county issues and other matters. It was a nice social time and I think it was good for all of us to get together outside of politics.

I served as Northwest District President for three terms (six years), which meant I also served on the AIC board for all of those years. I especially liked AIC because it encompassed all of the county officials, not just one group. I loved being active with clerk's and auditors, but I really learned a lot about county government in general by serving with so many different officeholders. My last year on the board, I served on the nominating committee and was asked to be an officer. Generally, the officers served in all of the 'chairs' and eventually became president. I would have loved that opportunity to serve as president of AIC, but I had decided by that time, not to run again for county office. Since I wouldn't be able to go all through the chairs, I didn't think it was fair to start and not finish. That was one of the few times that I regretted not continuing my county government career.

I think that the Association of Indiana Counties is probably one of the best professional organizations I know, or at least it was then. I have no reason to think the organization has changed. Over the years there were many changes in Executive Directors, which is not all that uncommon, and I liked, and worked well, with all of them. I was still serving on the board when we hired the current Executive Director, David Bottorff, who had worked as an aide in the Indiana House of Representatives. I don't remember the exact date he started, but that is a testament to the success of the organization. A great deal of that success is due to the competence and consistency David has brought to the helm, which shines through every day.

The AIC not only provided county officials with meetings and conferences to learn about the changes in legislation, they also encouraged all county officials to keep learning about their jobs in general. They instituted a program for continuing education called the "County D.I.P.L.O.M.A. Program." It stood for Development, Improvement, and Preparation for Leadership, Organizational, and Management Achievement. It was a two-year program with both core and elective courses. There was no state requirement—we weren't licensed nor did we need continuing education credits, but it was based on that format. It gave each officeholder an opportunity to add some credentials to their name, as well as be better at the many responsibilities the jobs required. It was a two-year program, and at the conclusion we were awarded certificates, you know, like a "diploma!"

The D.I.P.L.O.M.A. program got off to a bit of a rough start, but like all things, they worked through the problems and it became quite successful. One of the first ones I attended was on finance and budgeting. The speaker was a professor from Indiana State University, (my alma mater) so I thought it would probably be really helpful. Local budgets are hard, and the auditor really does the whole thing. Well after he got into his presentation, it became pretty obvious he had no practical knowledge at all; he was just reciting from some textbook. The auditors in the room were getting very 'antsy' because he kept giving outdated information. When he would say something wrong, we would all kind of quietly whisper "no, no, no", until a couple of the auditors said to me, "You need to tell him he is wrong or we will have a mess on our hands." I loved that, "YOU need to tell him." Why was it always ME who needed to tell everyone? But I did, as graciously and diplomatically as I could, point out to him that some of the information he was providing was no longer valid; that the statutes had been changed; and he might want to update his materials. Well, the AIC staff was very upset that he had done such a poor job (he wasn't even an interesting speaker) so they promised to hold another session and everyone in the room could take it at no charge. The sessions were not expensive, but we did pay to help offset the cost of the materials, and lunch was included. They did eventually hold another session on budgets, it was well attended, and the information was up to date and correct. This program was so successful that it continues today under another name. It is now called the AIC Institute for Excellence in County Government. Great new name, same great program.

I met some really terrific people while I was on the AIC Board and it is one of my fondest memories from my county government days. From time to time I check the AIC website (didn't have that when I was a board member) just to see what they are doing and how things have changed. It is a great organization and I would encourage every county official in the State of Indiana to participate and take advantage of what they have to offer.

The group of clerks who had worked on the single fee legislation. We were at our last state meeting together in 1990.

Me with the three other clerks 'turned' auditors. The four of us served sixteen years together.

County D.I.P.L.O.M.A. Program

Development
Improvement and
Preparation for
Leadership
Organizational and
Management
Achievement

1995 Continuing Education Certificate

Mary Lou Leavell, Auditor

Marshall County

_____
Sue Paris
President,
Association of Indiana Counties

October 1, 1995
Date

One of my certificates from the old D.I.P.L.O.M.A. program.

At a state Auditor's meeting having dinner with our good friend Ken Minot from SIECO. (Southern Indiana Engineering Company). First deputy Sharon Satorius is next to Ken, settlement deputy Neysa McFarland is next to me.

A group of auditors and vendors hanging out in the auditor's hospitality room. Often vendors would sponsor the room and 'work it' for us. Great bunch of people.

The view from the balcony of the lodge in Allen County. This was during one of our weekend clerk retreats. Great friends, great times.

Our first year at 'the lodge' after we all left the clerk's office and moved on to other county positions or careers. We were running around in a pumpkin patch!

Attending my last county commissioner meeting. The room was full of elected officials and department heads to wish me well. This is when I received my mantel clock. December 31, 1999.

Taken at the end of the day, my last day in office. I was with Neysa and Sharon, the two deputies who had been with me the longest, Sharon for all sixteen years and Neysa for fifteen years. I still miss them both.

Part 5 - Life After County Government

"What I have learned is that people become motivated when you guide them to the source of their own power and when you make heroes out of employees who personify what you want to see in the organization."

—Anita Roddick

Chapter 19
And Now, The End Is Near

The election for my successor in the auditor's office took place in 1998 because it was a holdover office. So I had to make some decisions about my future long before anything would change. There was a contingent out there, including my husband, who wanted me to run for clerk again. There had been so many changes in the clerk's office that I felt it might have been like starting over, not to mention a completely different staff. Of course, I could go back to that office and not have to give up my last year as auditor. If I ran for office and won, I could continue on the AIC board and become an officer, I would have liked that. There would be guaranteed job security for another four years, without the constraints of clocking in and out—although I worked many extra hours anyway. There were two things that kept me from running for office again: I didn't want to be one of those people who never knew when to quit and eventually get voted out of office; and I was collapsing under the stress.

My last few years in office were the most stressful years of the entire sixteen, even after having been accused of cheating on an election. That wasn't as stressful as this job had become. I had a county commissioner elected who had previously been a judge. We'd had a few 'go-arounds' when I was clerk, and he made my life miserable as auditor. First of all, he had no respect for the position I held, my experience, or the knowledge that went with it. He didn't really grasp that he was not in charge; that there were two other commissioners who deserved respect and consideration; and that all of the other officeholders also deserved respect.

Now I had known this man and his family for years and years. I had liked all of them. They were active Republicans, so we saw them at all the GOP events, not to mention just being active and involved in the community. So needless to say, I was flabbergasted at the way he treated the first female commissioner we ever had. She was young, about the same age as one of his daughters, but that shouldn't have mattered. I know that she was recruited by the sheriff to run against the Democrat commissioner (the one I liked and thought was the best we had). Unfortunately, those who recruited her did not really explain to her what the job was. I don't think she really had any idea how intense, time consuming, and complicated it is to be a county commissioner. She won of course, because she was a Republican, and because they ran a really ugly campaign against her opponent, whom she did not know, and later felt bad about. However, she did win, so there was no excuse for this commissioner to treat her like he did. Actually, I was surprised at his attitude—he had a very strong, independent wife, so I would have thought he'd respect a strong women. Wrong. He didn't respect her and he certainly didn't respect or even like me.

I spent hours and hours during her first year as commissioner coaching, teaching, and trying to help her understand the job. She wasn't stupid, she simply had no idea how county government worked and was up against two commissioners who didn't want her there and were not willing to help her. They were just more comfortable with having our board of commissioners made up of old white guys. I had been thrilled that we finally had a female commissioner, even though she beat my favorite guy, and was heartsick and angry at the way she was treated. Mr. Miserable would have been livid if someone had treated his daughter like that.

His refusal to work with me and his insistence to do everything on his own, left me in constant clean up mode of all the messes he made and the people he pissed off, not to mention a female commissioner who spent a great deal of her time in my office in tears of frustration. It all made an already very stressful time even worse. During her second year in office, she began to talk about resigning because he had made her so miserable. I begged her not to do that for two reasons; that is exactly what he wanted, and if she could hang in there until the end of her term, I would run for her spot since she lived in my district. But I couldn't convince her. She resigned that spring, and by that time I was in my last year of office. So I decided to throw my hat in the ring to be appointed to fill her vacancy. I didn't really want to give up the second half of my last year, but my successor had been elected, so he would be appointed to take over, and I could continue to work with him and train him while I served as a commissioner. Then I would run when that commissioner term was up.

It was a county-wide office so I contacted all of the GOP precinct people who I knew would be voting on that position. I told them I wanted to replace her and outlined my experience with the county; which all of them already knew. I expected others to put their names in too. The other candidates were all men. It is a whole lot easier to fill a vacancy than to be elected by the entire county, plus you then have an edge when you are required to run in the election. Unfortunately for me, one of the men who was running was recruited by the other two commissioners. He was the son of a former commissioner who had served for twenty years. He had lots and lots of name recognition. They did not want me appointed for three reasons: I knew way more about county government than the two of them would ever know; I would not be their puppet and do their bidding; and I would make them do everything right because I'm honest to a fault and I believe you either follow the rules, laws, and procedures, (especially your own), or change them. Even though I would have been terrific commissioner for Marshall County, they didn't care, they wanted another male so they could go back to being the good ol' boys and doing things their way.

Well, I did everything I was supposed to do, including prepare a really good speech for the caucus where her replacement would be chosen. I am the only one of all of the candidates who actually stood in front of the room and talked about the county and what it is all about. Nobody else could do that because nobody else knew it like I did. The rest of them got up and blathered about how important it was to 'stick together' and one of them even said he thought decisions should be made in a back room in private. Holy smokes, talk about setting the county up for lawsuits and liability—not to mention going back to the dark ages.

When you have worked with these Republican officials as much as I have, especially when I was clerk and conducting elections, it is pretty easy to read them. When I walked in the door of that caucus room and said hello, I knew immediately that I would probably not win. Very few of them looked me in the eye, even those from Plymouth whom I had known and worked with for thirty years. But I wasn't going down without a fight. There were four other candidates and it took five ballots before they had a winner. I hung in there on all five ballots, but their chosen 'boy' won the race. And all these years later he is still serving as a commissioner. I expect he will be one of those who never leaves, until he is forced to leave by the voters. That is a shame, because people who give a lot of years deserve to go out with pomp and celebration, not crawl away in defeat. But very few know that.

After the caucus, the press interviewed me and asked what I was going to do now. They acted like my life was over. Well good grief, I was only fifty years old—hardly dead. So I told them I would finish my term as auditor and then get on with life, I had lined up a job when my term ended so I would continue with my plans. What else could I say, I couldn't read tea leaves. In retrospect, it was probably better that I was not appointed, since my husband died right after my term ended and I really didn't need another county-wide campaign on my plate. Besides, I'm not sure I could have run and gotten elected that year without him, he had always been there for all of my campaigns. And I didn't really want to try.

After that decision was made, I went back to work and began the arduous task of dismantling my office. Cleaning out and organizing files; taking a lot of my personal stuff home,(with no clue what I was going to do with it), and trying my very best to interest my successor in coming in to learn the job. I knew he had a day job—after all it had been eleven months since the election and a man's gotta eat—and auditor is a tough job on the best of days. I had taken him to as many meetings as I could, but hands-on is really the best way to learn. I had even suggested he do what I did and take the previous year's ledger books home, along with the financial report, and study in his spare time. Nope, not interested. I began to have a sneaking suspicion that he would serve the same way a lot of my fellow male officeholders served—more as figurehead than as an actual doer of the work. Kind of normal for the boys.

During the first week of December, I attended my final commissioner's state meeting. That would be the last opportunity for me to meet with my fellow auditors, some of the vendors, and other county government people around the state. It was a bittersweet meeting for me. I knew there were some I might not see again, but I was also looking forward to my future. I had taken a job with a software company in South Bend that called on counties and schools. I was anxious to learn the software and continue to see and occasionally work with county officials I knew.

The Friday after the commissioner's meeting, my husband and I made plans to go to South Bend for dinner and a game of cards with our golfing friends. I knew it would be a busy month, ending my term, of course my last settlement, and getting ready for Christmas, etc. December in the auditor's office is always crazy busy. While we were in South Bend, Tom started not feeling well, so on the advice of our hostess who was a nurse, I took him to the hospital. That was good advice, he was having a heart attack. He never came home to Plymouth again.

On my last day in office, my staff had a small reception for me in the office. Since my husband was in the hospital on life support, they decided something a bit subdued would be best. I didn't know they were going to do that, so I was pleased at their decision. Many people who I had worked with over the years stopped by, some close friends came in and some political supporters were there. It was hard though, because this was just the type of thing my husband would have loved and he would have been right in the middle of it all. Of course, had he not been sick, there would have been a much bigger party.

By my last day, I had started letting my successor cover the commissioner meetings so I wasn't with them for their final meeting of the year. My first deputy came and got me and said they had a question. I went into the meeting and here was a whole room full of county officials and department heads to tell me goodbye. They presented my with a plaque, thanking me for my sixteen years of service to the county, and gave me a lovely mantle clock that chimes on the hour. I still have the clock; it is in my living room on a shelf. Many times when it chimes, I think back to that time of my life—what a special time it was; how lucky I was to have been able to serve my county for so many years; and to get to know all of the people throughout Indiana who I was fortunate enough to call my friends.

Chapter 20
Lessons Learned, and There Were Many

It would be pretty sad to think that someone who started a career at age thirty-two and finished that job at age fifty didn't learn something in those eighteen years. Of course, I did the obvious learning: went to the meetings, learned to read the Indiana Code Book and how to interpret the statutes. I'm not a lawyer and never pretended to be, but it is simply not practical to call an attorney every time you need to read a law—not to mention what that would do to the budget. I did, from time to time, ask one of my judges, and they were happy to help me. I paid close attention at the meetings, and took pretty good notes, although later, I wasn't always sure what my notes meant. But probably the most important thing I did was to pay attention. To everyone and everything. I watched how other people did things, and I asked questions of my fellow officeholders; sometimes at the meetings and sometimes I just called them. I remember when I was first auditor, I was struggling with one of the budget forms. I finally just called another auditor and she patiently walked me through it until the light bulb came on. From that point on, I totally understood how to do the budgets. It could have taken me forever, with many screw ups, if she hadn't been willing to help me. I continued to study and got better at my jobs clear up until the very end of both positions.

But there were some other lessons that were a little harder to learn. They weren't so obvious and my learning curve was developed by necessity. Here are a few of those lessons:

- No one is irreplaceable. No one. I learned that the hard way when I failed to fire the deputy clerk who lied to me. Not only was I unable to trust her, I think it probably damaged my reputation a little bit with the rest of my staff. No one ever said anything of course, but I always wondered if they thought I might be a bit of a coward. I think they would have been right.
- Women are harder to manage than men. Both of my successors in office were men; both were walking into offices staffed with women. Neither of them was at all prepared for that. I have already covered my experiences with staff, but one thing I told both of my successors—women take things personally. Neither of them listened to me. My successor in the clerk's office probably struggled with that the most because he had been a manager in his previous position, but only of men. There is a huge difference. Men can fight and argue about something having to do with work, then walk out the door and go get a drink like there is nothing wrong. I saw that all the time with the attorneys, and had that kind of relationship with two of my judges. Doesn't work that way with women. They get mad, and stay mad. Now, in comparison, I think that women are better workers. They do what needs to be done, they don't spend a lot of time trying to figure out how to get someone else to do it, like many of the men in my experience. If given the right guidance,

women will work hard, learn everything they can, do the job well, and meet the deadlines. Men, not so much. Women are also much more trusting, once you have won their trust. As I told both those guys, "You have to earn their loyalty and respect, they are not going to give it to you automatically. They will come in here and do the job, be nice to you, and help you. But if you want them to have your back, you better have theirs." Both of them had to learn that lesson the hard way. Should have listened to what this woman said about those women, I really did know what I was talking about.

- Know your stuff, you will be challenged on a daily basis. But if you don't know something, be big enough to say so and go find the answer. These are not jobs you can BS your way through. You might get away with that on the campaign trail, but not once you take office. These are very public jobs and there will always be people out there rooting for you to fail; so work smart, not stupid and you won't get caught looking stupid. Neither of them followed that advice either.

- Don't sell out, it isn't worth it. I couldn't really relay this advice to my successors, I didn't know them that well. I only know that it was important to me. I tried to serve every year as honestly and up front as I could. When someone asked me to cut a corner, which happened sometimes in election work or with rules and procedures for personnel, I refused. I wanted to help people in any way I could, but not by breaking rules and doing 'end arounds.' I always said that a huge part of my jobs, both of them, was putting out fires. People would often come into my office and ask for a way to accomplish something; maybe how to handle a grant with a different fiscal year than the county, or how to fill out a form or a finance report. Sometimes it was a member of the public; sometimes it was a candidate or precinct worker; sometimes it was a county employee or another elected official. I always did what I could to help them with their fire, but not if the only way was to bend or break the rules. I did not do that. I was, and still am, a straight shooter. It drove a lot of people crazy, but they could always count on me to steer them in the right direction. They didn't have to take my advice or do it my way if they didn't want to, but if they did, they wouldn't get in trouble.

- If you screw up, admit it, fix it, apologize, and move on. There is nothing more frustrating for me than when people ask to be in a position of leadership, i.e., run for office, then get the job and decide it is really hard and really public. Well surprise, surprise, what did they think it would be? All of these jobs were hard, some harder than others for sure, but they all had responsibilities that were important and affected other people's lives. Whether it is the challenge of being the boss, or conducting a meeting, or making big decisions, it is hard. It is hard precisely because no matter what you do, you cannot please everyone. Abraham Lincoln told us that over one hundred years ago. And public office is the classic job wherein there is no way to keep everyone happy. So, you do your best. And if you make a mistake, suck it up, apologize, then fix it. If your staff makes a mistake, accept that you are in charge, take the heat, apologize, then fix it. And then deal with your staff person in private (but especially not in the newspaper).

- If you are a woman and lucky enough to be tall, wear high heels. Most men are short. When I started in the clerk's office, I realized my biggest challenge was going to be getting the attorneys and judges to take me seriously. Men will take you seriously if they have to look up at you, or at least eye to eye. Of course there were a few tall attorneys, but I was five feet, eight inches tall, so add two or three inch heels, and I was up there with the best of them. And it worked.

Of course, all these years later, I look back and know that there were still some lessons I probably didn't learn—I can be stubborn. And I no longer wear high heels. Ever. But for the most part I feel that I traversed my sixteen years of challenges—the public, my colleagues, my staff, all the decisions I had to make—and I think I followed my own rules pretty well. I didn't cause the county any heavy duty lawsuits, I didn't go to jail, I won a few awards, and I lived to tell the story.

Not bad for a thirty-two year old kid who was just looking for a job with decent pay.

Chapter 21
Movin' On Down the Road

There is something to be said for having lived at the change of a century. Although, Y2K turned out to not be the end of the world like so many thought it would be, it was still a big change for me. I spent that New Year's Eve, the night of my last day in office, with some friends, and my son. We had dinner, played some cards, and generally just chatted, mostly about my husband. And three days later he died. Eighteen days earlier he had turned fifty-seven years old.

Of course, he and I had made all kinds of plans for our time after I left office. I was looking forward to my new job. They had hired me for my county government experience and my knowledge of payroll. They were in the process of writing a new payroll program and wanted me to sell it and train people on it. I enjoyed doing both, so I thought it was a pretty good fit.

We had agreed to the arrangement the previous October, even though I wouldn't start until January. Some of their customers were in southern Indiana, and I was going to try to arrange it out so that when I needed to go that far away, Tom would go with me. We would try to arrange those trips on a Thursday or Friday, throw the golf clubs in the car, and maybe stay over the weekend and play golf. He was not ready to retire, but was thinking of taking a bit more time off. It was a great plan.

I had made arrangements to take off the first two weeks of January. I would receive my last check from the county in January, so I wanted to take a break before I started the new job. Of course those two weeks turned out to be completely different than I had anticipated in October. I had never expected a funeral to be part of my immediate future.

I started my new job, but realized shortly after that I shouldn't have. After all, I was only fifty years old, I needed a job, I thought I couldn't go without a paycheck. My husband had just died, I was by myself. Also, this job in South Bend brought something else new to me—a commute. To be there at 8:00 AM meant leaving my house absolutely no later than 7:00AM. Now, county offices opened at 8:00AM, but I was no more than fifteen minutes away, from my house, so I never had to leave that early. Another unexpected change was that I came home every single day to an empty house with only the dog happy to see me. I was really glad I had him, at least there was a living creature there talk to. It was a real struggle for me, but I didn't know what else to do. I had to work, and I felt like I had to give this job a try. The people I would be working for were very nice and understanding; it was a family business and their mother had just died a few months before that. But I couldn't concentrate. I had no idea that was a classic sign of grief. I didn't know anything about grief; what to expect; what it felt like; how I would react. I guess I thought I would just carry on without much change. It just doesn't work that way.

As it turned out, I never really settled into the job. I did okay when I was out traveling and calling on customers, or training them, but there were more days in the office than travel days, and I was miserable in my little cubicle, and there was still the confinement of eight-to-five with only thirty minutes for lunch. Tom had warned me I would hate that, he had been right, I did hate that. Eventually I convinced them to let me work part of the time from home, but that wasn't much better.

After coming home one time and collapsing in tears in front of my sister, she convinced me I needed to give up that job and find something closer to home. So I went to work for another company that consulted with counties on their tax sales. Tax sales are what happens when a property owner doesn't pay their taxes. After a certain amount of delinquency, their property goes up for 'tax sale.' Some properties are very nice and can be purchased at a really good price. The auditor and treasurer work together regarding tax sales, but it wasn't something I personally did very much as auditor, so I wasn't that knowledgeable about them. But the fellow who hired me was a former auditor friend, and he knew that my previous county government experience and contacts would be an asset. I told him I would give it a try and work on a part-time basis. One of the things I loved most about that job was that they sold to auditors, so I got to see all my old friends at the state meetings. Of course they came to my vendor booth, and during the off hours I just hung out with them. That part was wonderful.

Several years prior to this time, my oldest sister had gotten a divorce. Part of her therapy for dealing with that was to participate in a group called Beginning Experience. It was a healing group for people who were single through death, divorce, or separation. They did weekend retreats, so it was very intense. She had shared a lot of her BE experiences with my family, so when Tom died, I asked her if I should go to a BE weekend. She said she would let me know when I was ready. Much later that year, in August, I received an envelope in the mail and all it had in it was an application to a BE weekend. No letter, no note, nothing. I guess she thought I was ready. I filled it out and went to the weekend.

It was very rewarding and helped me meet people who were going through what I was going through. One of those people was a young man whose wife had been killed in a car accident. He was really struggling and looking for answers anywhere he could find them. One day, he told me about an online grief support group called WidowNet. Well, I was only a mediocre computer user, but I gave it a try. There were lots of stories from different people, from all over the country. One of those stories was from a gentleman in Minnesota who was talking about his business suffering after his wife died. Well, I had been thinking of starting a business, so I sent him an email and asked him some questions. Long story short, he was originally from Indiana, his name is Tom. We got to know each other, then got to know each other very well. As of now we have been married nineteen years. (I only marry men named Tom—makes my life easier).

When we were first married, we moved to Minnesota because I was mobile and he really wasn't. Before I made the move permanent, I was back in Indiana finishing up my job with the tax sale consultant when September 11 happened. He was in Minnesota, I was in Indiana, both of us were watching all of that on television, by ourselves, and it was horrible. I decided right then and there, I was moving to Minnesota and not coming back without him.

A couple of years later, the contract work he had done for the Minneapolis Park Board ended so we had to make some decisions. We decided to leave Minnesota and head for someplace warm. I had previously vacationed in North Carolina and loved it. We chose Durham, North Carolina. We lived in Durham for four years, and during that time I worked at a software company in Raleigh; another company that catered to city and county governments. They hired me for my county government experience, then became frustrated with me because I was not a computer programmer. I hung in there for a year and a half, then said, "Screw it." It was a sixty minute commute and it just wasn't worth it.

While we were in Durham, I convinced my new husband to get back into music. Tom is a professional musician and vocalist, and he had backed away from music while his late wife was sick. I felt like he had too much talent and experience to not use it, so I encouraged him to find someplace he could play. It took a bit of adjustment on my part; I was used to a nine-to-five life, Monday through Friday. Musicians work nights and weekends.

He began to substitute with the Raleigh Jazz Orchestra until they asked him to be their regular drummer. Through the RJO, he met several musicians and began to think about 'resurrecting' his band from Minnesota. He found enough guys who wanted to play that style of music, and started another music career.

In the meantime, I tried to get involved in politics, and actually applied for a job with the Durham County election office. I had an interview with the election director, but he was convinced my previous experience as a boss would not allow me to be a good employee. I kept telling him I had no interest in being in charge; I just loved election work. But no dice. I guess he was afraid of a strong, capable woman. Not much I can do to change that.

After a few years, I began to feel frustrated with Durham, I'm a small town girl and it is a pretty good sized city. I met some folks at one of Tom's concerts who talked about how much they loved Pinehurst. They had retired there from Michigan and were so glad they did. We decided to check it out, so one Saturday in October we drove down to Moore County and drove all through Pinehurst and Southern Pines. We both fell in love with Southern Pines, so we went back to Durham, sold our home, bought a patio home in Southern Pines, and moved in May of 2007. It has been our home ever since.

Again, I tried to get involved in county government, this time in Moore County. On two different occasions they listed an opening for a job called "Clerk to the County Commissioners", I applied for it both times and never even got an interview. North Carolina local governments have city and county managers. So I just went in one day, on the advice of a current county commissioner whom I had met, and introduced myself to the county manager. I gave him a copy of my resume and told him I was interested in part-time work wherever he could use me. When I was in office I would have loved to have someone with my experience show up and offer to 'fill in' where needed. But he was borderline rude, and I'm sure when I left he threw my resume away.

So I gave up on county government and moved in another direction. I ended up working at an historical hotel in downtown Southern Pines. It has fifteen rooms and has been completely renovated. It was beautiful, and I really enjoyed that job—I was the 'concierge' of the charming town of Southern Pines. I worked there for five years until my granddaughter was born, then I wanted the freedom to go back and forth to Charleston and be Grandma. I finally retired from my retirement job.

In the meantime Tom continued building his music career, for at least the second time. He played with the musicians he met in

Raleigh and took every gig he could find. It paid off and he became known as one of the best drummers in the whole area. While building his music business, he decided to try teaching private music lessons. He had never thought of himself as a teacher, but I convinced him that since he was a bit older—and should be a bit more patient—teaching might be something he enjoyed, He signed up to teach at a new music store in town, and then joined a private teaching studio with a guitar teacher, piano teacher, and vocal teacher. Eventually, they all moved on, so he opened a studio in downtown Southern Pines, and his business grew to the point where he often has a waiting list.

He was with a local church, playing drums in their newly formed contemporary service band. He played for them until the music director left the church. He was subsequently hired to take her place as the Praise Band Director and has made great strides with the band. He really enjoys this gig; it's right here in town and it's a 'sit down' gig (drums are always there and always set up). The people of the church have been wonderful to both of us and we eventually made the decision to join and become full members.

We have created a wonderful, full life all these years later. Tom is into music full time, I love being retired and doing what I want, especially spending time with my grandchildren. I am active in my community and in my church, as I have always been. We play golf together, spend time on our beautiful screened porch and deck together, do church together, and continue aging together. We are truly enjoying our life.

As of this writing we have lived in North Carolina for seventeen years, in Southern Pines for thirteen of those years. In December of 1999, I would never have envisioned my life would go in this direction after I left county government. But that just goes to show, we never know where life will take us. I guess the best thing to do is just be ready for whatever happens. I tried to face and accept my new life with courage, flexibility, and most of all, a sense of humor. So far it has worked, I love my life and hope it lasts as I move on down that (hopefully) long, long road.

Chapter 22:
Life After Party Politics, Who Knew?

After we moved to Southern Pines, I decided that I no longer wanted to be involved in politics. I didn't like the direction the political scene was taking; more and more polarized; meaner and meaner campaigns; 'say-and-do-anything-to-win' mentality. Also, I was watching the Tea Party and ultra right wing take over my party. I voted as a Republican for a few years, and helped on a local campaign, but eventually I changed my voter registration to unaffiliated. That is a type of voter registration in North Carolina and I felt that suited me better.

Even though I was out of politics, I never lost my love of local government, nor lost sight of how important good local government is to a community. So I decided to join The League of Women Voters of Moore County. Back during my first year or two as clerk, some of us tried to get a League started in Marshall County. Mary B and I, plus a Republican woman and a Democrat woman, hosted an organizational meeting at the library. We had a pretty good turnout, but we just could never garner enough interest to make it happen. So I was really pleased when I found a very active league in Moore County.

I didn't know much about the League, but I started going to their meetings, making friends with other members, and helping where I could. Not long after I joined there was a vacancy on their Board of Directors, so they asked me to fill that spot. I did, because I thought it would give me a good opportunity to really learn how it worked. I had only attended a couple of board meetings when there was another vacancy. You guessed it, secretary. I tried to slide down in my chair so they wouldn't remember I was there, but it didn't work and the next thing I know I'm taking minutes. How in the world did that happen? I am so easy.

Over the next year, as I attended the board meetings and regular meetings, I got to know more and more people. One day, after a regular monthly meeting, our treasurer, the late Ginger Finney, asked me if I would consider being fund-raising chair. If so, she would be on the committee with me. Fund-raising chair. What on earth did I know about fund raising? I wasn't any good at fund-raising for my own campaigns, let alone for an organization. But I told her I would think about it and see if I could come up with some ideas.

And I did. A pretty good idea, actually. As a matter of fact, we are still doing this project and have raised almost $50,000 in twelve years. Plus, the project has been so popular that we have also taken in lots and lots of new members. I don't know for sure how many, but over the last few years our membership has nearly doubled.

My idea? *"Lunch With Legends."* I was working around the house one day, doing a little cleaning, and while I was dusting my bookshelf I noticed a book Tom had given me for Christmas. It was entitled *Women's Letters: A female Perspective On America Through Letters that Women have Written from the Revolutionary War to the Present* (2005). I looked at the book and began to think about having a presentation that portrayed those women reading their letters, in period costumes, as part of a ladies luncheon. I wanted something that reflected what the League was about. Style shows and bridge tournaments are fine, but we are more than that, we are about civic engagement and responsibility. So I decided to portray first ladies. I asked Tom if he would be my emcee, and maybe sing, and he said yes. So I began to formulate how this might work.

I went to the League board and presented my idea. They liked the idea, but one lady asked if I would consider diversity. Well, of course that was a wonderful idea; it didn't have to be first ladies. Besides, not all of them made much of an impact. I wanted to have this event in March, because that is Woman's History Month. The board approved the project and told me to run with it.

So Ginger and I got busy. She took care of the venue, the menu and the ticket sales. I wrote the scripts and developed the program. The first year, I wanted to celebrate a woman from each century of America's history; the eighteenth century, the nineteenth century, and the twentieth century. And there was one other other criteria—they all had to be dead. So I picked Abigail Adams, Carrie Chapman Catt, and Eleanor Roosevelt. A lot of people don't realize that Abigail was a huge advocate of rights for women and girls, especially in the area of education. Carrie was the founder of the League of Women Voters, and Eleanor—well, we all know the zillion accomplishments of Eleanor.

I started researching my ladies to see what I could find to make it interesting. I decided that I needed a back story for each of them to go along with the well-known facts of their accomplishments. I wrote the scripts in two parts; first person and third person. When the ladies were speaking, they spoke in first person and shared their personal experiences, opinions, etc. The third person part was read by a narrator—my husband, Tom. I liked the idea of a man's voice, especially his beautiful, easy-to-understand baritone voice, to contrast with the female voices. As I completed each script, I asked Tom to proofread them and give me his opinion. He is also a published writer, so he had a lot of credibility with me. He read them, he made some minor changes and suggestions, and when they were completed he said, "Well, my dear, I believe you have just written three screenplays." Well, damn. Who knew I could do that?

I picked the League members I wanted to portray my ladies, and gave them their scripts to practice. We did this as readers' theater, but it still takes a lot of practice; they needed to be very, very familiar with the script. Each one dressed in period costumes; Eleanor even found a fox collar. Since Tom was the narrator for all three characters, he couldn't be in costume (no time to change) so instead, I had him change his hat to reflect the period. He wore a tricorn hat with Abigail, a top hat with Carrie, and a fedora with Eleanor. It helped him progress through the eras of the program and the crowd loved it.

There was a committee of only three that year: me; Ginger (the treasurer who had recruited me), and our president Jo Nicholas; and really, we would have to add Tom to the committee. He designed and printed all of the programs, the advertising, and the tickets. We were all sweating bullets, hoping to sell one hundred and twenty-five tickets to cover costs. So imagine our surprise when we sold one hundred and seventy-five tickets. The lunch was really good, the audience loved the presentations, and Tom sang a couple of patriotic songs at the end, of course the audience went nuts for that, he has a gorgeous voice.

We made nearly fifteen hundred dollars on that first effort and we were ecstatic. The project took off and I have since written nineteen biographical scripts and, in honor of the Centennial celebration of the passage of the nineteenth amendment, I wrote two one-act plays for the 2019 and 2020 Legends programs. In 2013, Tom and I decided it would be a good idea to start selling ads for the program books. He printed the books and was willing to insert the ads; he even created some logos for our advertisers. That increased the profit considerably and the League determined that the project was a keeper. In 2016, the League started to really concentrate on selling ads. Around that time, the board decided to start a scholarship program for high school students who were interested in pursuing public service of some kind. The committee was formed and the first recipients were introduced at the 2017 Lunch With Legends.

After the 2015 Legends, I decided it was time for someone else to step in and write the scripts. I had been the author since our maiden voyage in 2009 and was feeling a bit burned out. Plus, I was teaching an adult tap class on Tuesdays and that interfered with League meetings. And finally, my mother got sick and died that year, and my son Steve was having some issues, so I thought it was time for me to back off and concentrate on my family. I did continue to pay my dues, but I didn't make it to the next two Legends events that I did not write. In 2018, the League invited Tom and I to be their guests at Legends for the tenth anniversary of the project. We were introduced and were given a lovely plaque. I thought my days as a Legends author were over; the torch had been passed. Well, no, not quite yet.

In early 2019, I received a call from one of the co-chairs of the Legends project. She asked me if I would write a special program honoring the first woman's rights convention in Seneca Falls, New York. She really, really, wanted me to do it. I wasn't sure what I would do; how I would write it or stage it, but the little hamster in my brain started on that wheel and the ideas just kept coming. I started by researching the convention and everything I could find about Seneca Falls; and a script began to form. I thought in the beginning, I might try to recreate the event, but decided that was too much work for a one act play. Instead, I decided to introduce the key players of the convention: Elizabeth Cady Stanton; Lucretia Mott, Frederick Douglas (the only man to ever be a "Legend"); and a surprise historical figure—an Iroquois Indian. I included a narrator to pull it all together and began rehearsals.

This was not reader's theater; only the narrator was able to read her script. Also, there was no way to stage it on the single riser like we had used for the previous presentations. So my sweet, producer husband got busy, and we 'built' a mini stage. He put up his band lights, used his cordless mics, and became my tech guy. Because there was so much dialog Tom found an open-source teleprompter program and loaded it on my computer. We used his computer monitors and I learned how to run the teleprompter so the cast was all set; they didn't have to try and memorize all those lines. They came up with their own costumes and, voila', we had a play. It was a great success and I was very pleased.

After Legends, Tom and I were sitting on our porch one evening and I began talking about the upcoming centennial—the one hundredth anniversary of the nineteenth amendment: woman's right to vote. After so many years of researching and writing about women who made a huge difference in our country, (many of them who were suffragists), plus researching and writing about Seneca Falls, I knew we needed to celebrate this in a big, big way. So he and I came up with some ideas. Then I went to the Board of Directors again and presented our ideas: An opening event in January, with a free screening of the HBO movie, *Iron Jawed Angels* at our historical theater in downtown Southern Pines; a costumed presentation of the suffrage movement with a Power Point slide program to take around to community organizations; a float in area parades featuring 'the silent sentinels' who picketed the White House; and finally, and old fashioned twenties-style garden party at a historical venue in Southern Pines that has gorgeous gardens and landscaping. The board loved the ideas and said 'run with it.' You know, every time you come up with the ideas, you also become chair of the event! So, I pulled together a committee of leaguers who were interested and we began to meet. They thought we should add a reception after the movie and I agreed that was a great idea.

A couple of us began to line up the venues for these events. We secured the Weymouth Center for the garden party, the Sunrise Theater for the movie, then wanted another historic building downtown for the reception immediately following the movie. We tried the few that were available but they were either too expensive or, in one case it was city owned, so we couldn't serve alcohol. I decided to wait and see if we could come up with something else. Then, on a whim, I checked with the historical hotel where I had worked. The owner didn't generally do that sort of thing, but I asked if we could use the space, and we would have a cash bar so he would get that revenue. He doesn't serve meals, so we would bring in our own snacks and I promised we would clean it all up. We would be in and out in a couple of hours, and this would be on a Wednesday evening, which is a slow bar night anyway. He agreed and we were set. We decided to have a 'suffrage march', with signs and all, from the theater to the hotel (it was only a block and a half).

Eventually the event expanded to include the traveling suffrage display from the North Carolina Archives, which they brought to the Southern Pines library, right across the parking lot from the theater. It included the original nineteenth amendment that had been sent to each state, as well as photographs of the women of North Carolina who were so active in the movement. It was really, really, neat. We invited the photographer from the local paper to come and take pictures and he loved it. He came to the theater before the movie started and, with the league members dressed in their suffrage white and big hats, and he was blown away. Then he came back after the movie to take pictures of the march and again, was blown away. We had some really, really cool publicity pictures after that event. We even got the town council to sign a resolution declaring it Suffrage Day in Southern Pines.

In December of 2019, I began to think about the 2020 Lunch With Legends and what I was going to do to 'finish' the story. Again, I started researching and reading, and decided I would start with the last ten years of the movement, with the key players telling their story. My characters were Carrie Chapman Catt, Alice Paul, Gertrude Weil, the founder of the North Carolina League and a suffragist, along with Josephine Dodge, an anti-suffragist. I used the same cast as the previous year; they were all very good, they were comfortable with the teleprompter, and I liked the idea of a continuing story. We rebuilt the stage, only we included a backdrop of the signs used in our march from the theater to the reception, and we didn't have Frederick. The cast outdid themselves with great costumes; they rehearsed and rehearsed here at my house; and after the performance it was declared a smashing hit! Bravo ladies.

For our traveling presentation I had written the story of the suffrage movement and Tom put together a wonderful slide presentation of historical pictures and video to go along with it. It was written for two people, dressed as suffragists, and we started presenting that to organizations in September of 2019. Our plan was to present it throughout our anniversary year of 2020. We also decided to add an encore Legends presentation of Seneca Falls and The Rest of the Story, at a special showing on August 26, 2020. That would be in the evening, with both stories combined into a two-act play. We would not charge very much, but use the income to fund the centennial activities. Our *Lunch With Legends* was held on March 10, and two days later the world shut down for the coronavirus pandemic. We were lucky we got it in, but our upcoming presentations were canceled; the upcoming parades were canceled; and our encore Legends presentation and garden party were postponed until 2021. Time will tell.

Over the years I have been very active in the League. In addition to Legends, I talked them into selling flag scarves as a fund raiser. I served as chair of the Voter Services committee. I served as a delegate at two national conventions; one in Portland, Oregon and one in Atlanta. We sold our scarves in Atlanta and that was cool, seeing all our scarves on the convention floor. The convention took place right around Flag Day, so everyone was eager to buy them.

The League of Women Voters has been a huge focus for me since I left county government and moved to North Carolina. However, I also taught tap dancing to senior ladies for ten years. I did my share of serving on the board of our homeowners association, and planned many activities for them. I am active in our church, and serve on the hospitality committee. My main job is to oversee the Sunday morning coffee and refreshments each week. And of course, I spend as much time as I can in Charleston with my grands, Olivia and Thomas, and their parents.

I have had some changes in my life that never would have occurred to me during all those years I was serving in office. For example: I never dreamed I would ever live anywhere but in Indiana; I never dreamed I would leave the Republican party because it had changed so much (actually I think the GOP left me); I never dreamed I would leave the Catholic Church and become a Methodist; and I certainly never dreamed I would ever be married to a musician; a man with incredible talent and ability, and he has encouraged and pushed me into creative endeavors I never would have thought possible.

It really didn't take me long to learn that there is life after county government. And in my case, a very new life. It sure has been an adventure, and hopefully with much more to come.

Tom and I on our wedding day, August 26, 2001

Our new combined family. TJ in the back, Tom and I, Steve, and Laura in the front. October 2001 at St. Mary's at Notre Dame where Laura went to college.

Our growing family, on our back deck in Southern Pines, Thanksgiving, 2016. Laura and her husband Matt, Steve, Me, Tom, Jerilyn and TJ sitting with brand new Thomas and two-year old Olivia.

My very special grands. At our house on Easter morning, 2019, before heading off to church.

On a visit to their house in Charleston before Covid kept everyone separated.

On their first day of school—finally getting to go back. Olivia into Kindergarten and Thomas into Pre-school.

League of Women Voters of Moore County
presents
Lunch with Legends
... an afternoon with historic women

Our Lunch With Legends Logo. Tom developed it for the 2009 Legends and it has been our logo and symbol ever since.

Our first LWL cast. Left to Right: Eleanor Roosevelt (Dot Greenwood), Carrie Chapman Catt (Jo Nicholas), and Abigail Adams (Mary Price), me, and Tom, the narrator.

Me with my friend, the late Ginger Finney. Ginger is the one who talked me into being fund raising chairman, but jumped right in and helped me pull it off. I couldn't have done it without her, and our president, Jo Nicholas.

The cast of our 2020 LWL—The Rest of the Story. Left to Right: Carrie Chapman Catt (Carolyn Mealing), Gertrude Weil (Marcey Katzman), Josephine Dodge (Mindy Fineman), and Alice Paul (Janet Samuelson). Weil was the founder and first president of the North Carolina League and Dodge was an avid 'anti-suffragist.'

My tappers—'Alive and Clickin' at a gig in Whispering Pines. One of twenty-five dance routines, including seven Christmas dances, and all the requisite costume accessories to go with them. I led this group for ten years.

Tom, doing what he does so incredibly well, singing and playing the drums, always at the same time. And he tries to convince me he is a single threader! Not with both hands and both feet on the drums, running the sound, and singing, all at the same time. Remarkable.

Tom and I when we joined the Pinehurst United Methodist Church. Never figured I would ever be a Methodist, but here I am. Tom is the leader of the PUMC 'Connections' Band and the contemporary service. Great people at PUMC, we are really happy there.

EPILOGUE

I hope you have enjoyed reading about my time in county government as much as I have enjoyed writing about it. I started out very young; realized I had lots to learn; did my best to learn it; and tried very, very hard to stay true to myself through it all.

I know I made mistakes, hindsight has proven that. But everything I did was done 'to the best of my ability'—just like I swore in my oaths. I tried to serve the people of Marshall County, Indiana with honesty, integrity, energy, impartiality, and competence.

I hope, when you have an occasion to do business with your own local government officials, wherever you live, you will remember that most of them are hard working folks, just like you, serving their citizens, 'to the best of their ability.'

Please treat them with respect, and even better, thank them.

Made in the USA
Monee, IL
03 November 2020